Livin' the Dream

LIVIN' THE DREAM

BY

FORMER CORRECTIONS OFFICER

JACK MCKRAKEN

ANTELOPE HILL PUBLISHING

Cover art by Swifty.
Edited by Coach Finstock.
Formatted by Margaret Bauer.

The author can be contacted at:
jack_mckraken@activist.com
Instagram @mckraken.books

Antelope Hill Publishing
www.antelopehillpublishing.com

Paperback ISBN-13: 978-1-956887-41-9
EPUB ISBN-13: 978-1-953730-48-0

This book is dedicated to Billy, Sean, Michael, Chris, Jimmy, Vinny, Rob, Chris, Sean, Randy, Andy, and Nick. You're alpha.

And to the hundreds of Corrections Officers across the nation who commit suicide every year. You may have taken your own lives, but we know who guided your hand. You are not forgotten.

CONTENTS

INTRODUCTION

A few words from author to reader

*B*ang! I had barely woken up, and already I was being assaulted by sounds of chaos from down the corridor. A quick glance revealed a worst-case scenario: just feet away from my desk were two Corrections Officers and a Sergeant manhandling a six-foot-five inmate who had no intention of cutting them any slack. I knew the convict.

Gang member.

Rapist.

Their shouts and screams echoed down the concrete halls, filling my ears with the all-too-familiar symphony of struggle. I listened closely, but the cacophony was too wild to capture. So I settled for what snippets I could make out amidst the confusion. "Stop resisting." "Racist-ass." "Kill your family!"

I rose from my desk and hustled to assist in any way I could. My post that day was the infirmary, a place that was usually a cakewalk, but today was breaking the mold from the start. The writhing bodies of my co-workers struggled to restrain the inmate. Both sides struck each other wildly in fury, and while the officers settled for body-holds and applying pressure to subdue the criminal, the criminal had no such reservations of his own. He punched and kicked and snapped with pearly fangs into any flesh available. He was bleeding from the eye, evidence of an earlier struggle I hadn't seen. At that moment, he was an animal, and the officers were his prey.

As I approached the brawl, the Sergeant held out his hand and told me to stop.

"Open the pen!" he said. Instantly, I knew what he wanted.

Not far from where they stood was a small, secure observation room used for medical purposes. We called it "the pen." In times of desperation, it was used to store an unruly convict until he cooled off. I grabbed hold of my jingling key-ring, fiddled with the lock, and swung the heavy door wide open. The officers didn't waste any time.

In one tremendous push, the trio of disheveled warriors used every ounce of their strength to manhandle the convulsing convict into the pen's maw. Each step was a struggle, their black boots stomping across gleaming tile in defiance of the convict's rage. The moment the inmate's body cleared the entrance to the pen, the officers gave a great heave, and I slammed the door shut and locked it instantly with a *click*.

Bam! Bam! Bam!

The convict slammed his open palms onto the surface of the door and the riot glass, leaving behind handprints of blood. He was cursing up a storm, and while he may have been physically contained, his rage was as free as a bird. The officers stepped back and caught their breath, tending to their disheveled uniforms.

"What the hell happened?" I asked, clipping the keys back onto my belt and looking at the Sergeant for insight.

"He's high," said the Sergeant. "Doped up on Fentanyl. He didn't want to take a piss test, and all of a sudden exploded. Said he was going to kill himself or us. Whichever came first."

"Fuck," I whispered. "What now?"

"He can't stay in there as-is. He threatened to kill himself, so now we have to strip him down and give him a bed and suicide smock, slippers, all that shit. But we need backup."

"You mean we're going back in there?" I asked, despite knowing the answer.

"Yep," the Sergeant deadpanned as he unclipped his radio and barked a few short verbal commands. Within minutes, the elevator that served our area opened with a distinct beep. Outran six other officers and the watch commander, a Lieutenant, each one eager to join the fray.

I glanced at the con trapped inside the pen. He had heard the elevator beep and the drumbeat of boots rounding the corner. Most men would have stood down at the sound of serious reinforcements. But this one? He merely smiled.

"Radu! Listen buddy, we gotta come in and strip you down. You know how the process works. We've done this be-"

"Hey fuck you, man!" Radu responded, slamming his fists on the riot glass and sending blood and spittle all over the pen. "I'mma fuckin' kill yo faggot ass! I know y'all play these fuckboi games. Y'all need ten niggas to fuck wit' one."

The Lieutenant looked to the Sergeant, and the Sergeant looked to us.

"Okay boys, we're going in," he said, folding his arms, face red and sweaty. "We got the camera?"

There were silence and some embarrassment. During the commotion, no one in the response team brought the most critical piece of equipment—the camcorder. In Corrections, designating someone to be the cameraman during a "use-of-force" or any other potentially violent interaction with a belligerent inmate was standard procedure. This incident was no different.

One of the responders, a thin, bespectacled officer in his late fifties by the name of Boney, volunteered to go back and retrieve it. And so we waited. And waited. The convict used the time to taunt his enemies through the glass. He cursed their families and mocked their appearances. He cast his doubts on our collective sexual orientation, and as he screamed and wailed and slammed his fists on the walls and windows, the heat that emanated from his pitch-black flesh and animalistic snarling caused the glass to fog with condensation. There was a battle about to unfold, but only one side would be allowed to treat it as such.

Finally, Boney returned with the camcorder. He and a few others started fiddling with the settings as best they could but struggled to turn the damn thing on. The convict found this a source of great hilarity. When one officer finally had enough, he gave the camera to the next man, and so on...each failing nonetheless. Finally, a younger officer gave it a try. Within moments he was able to identify the problem: there was no SD card inserted. There was a collective groan, and the Sergeant, knowing this was his operation, grew redder by the minute. The Watch Commander merely held his head in humiliation.

"You dumb! Y'all niggas is dumb!" crowed Radu.

The officers, myself included, were growing angrier. In a normal world, we would open the door and let this piece of filth have it. But in the upside-down world of State Corrections, we were hamstrung by policy. We were neutered of true authority. We were held back out of fear of legal retaliation. Worst of all: The inmate knew it, and he used that knowledge well.

As we waited, we took our verbal lashings from the convict, embarrassment setting in. But before morale suffered any more damage, Boney finally returned. In his hands was the essential SD card. He gave it to the younger officer, who deftly inserted it and began filming the pen.

Everyone steeled themselves. It was go time.

Once the order was given, I cracked the door. Through the gap rushed a mass of uniformed force, approaching their target with the furious eyes of scorned men. They slammed their bodies into the convict, pinning him against the concrete walls of the pen and holding him tightly in place. Despite their numerical superiority, the convict bucked and resisted, sending the combatants sprawling on the floor and turning a vertical fight into a horizontal one.

Blood pooled on the ground and splattered onto my shirt and arms. "I got AIDS! I got AIDS!" he screamed, laughing as he thrashed. The air filled with the grunts and groans of struggle, but also with the thumps of wooden batons, still hanging limply at the officers' sides. In Corrections, they were for show. Fear of legal reprisals had turned the once-essential baton into nothing more than a visual reminder, an ornamental showpiece. It was odd that officers still carried them at all.

The human pile that had formed on the inmate's back was reaching its limit of effectiveness, and I found myself devoting my entire body weight to holding down a single kicking leg. The struggle lasted another few minutes, and then the inmate suddenly stopped. He gave in: too tired to continue the fight, too exhausted to sustain the ridicule. Once the worst was over, the Sergeant took over, commanding his number one man to remove the inmate's clothes and administer a suicide smock, per Departmental procedure. The rest of us filed out, and I once again locked the door behind me.

The brass sat around in the infirmary for a while, making sure the inmate was properly cared for. It was a madhouse. Personnel from throughout the facility swung by out of morbid curiosity, wondering what could have happened so early in the shift to cause the response team to vanish from their units and regular posts. I washed my hands of prison blood and requested to go to medical to get checked out. The Sergeant shook his head and assured me that I was fine. Frustrated, I sat back down at my desk and resumed filling out the logbook, a chore I hadn't had time to deal with since the fight erupted. As I scribbled a frenzied passage into those crumpled pages, the phone to the unit rang.

"McKraken, Infirmary." I answered, rolling my eyes.

"McKraken, it's Wannamaker." Replied the officer on the other end. "Bro, we heard what happened; how is everyone up there? You guys okay?"

"Okay?" I scoffed. "We're fine. We're just living the dream."

* * *

Picture this: you live in the middle of nowhere. Your neighbors are distant, the weather is all over the map, and the closest sign of civilization is a strip mall thirty miles down the highway. If you're lucky, you managed to finish high school, and now that you're ready to enter the workforce, you quickly discover that your only job prospects are either McDonald's or the Army.

This somewhat hopeless scenario is pretty much what it's like to live in New York. That's State, not City. There's a vast social nothingness to the north and west of the richest and most degenerate place in the western world, and while it's filled with natural beauties, it lacks the pleasures that a more metropolitan life offers. There's more to "New York" than Rockefeller Center, Times Square, and Williamsburg. Yes, people *actually* live in areas of New York outside the city limits. There are millions of people out there in forgotten rural areas all over the country, just like me, who once stared the "McDonald's-Army" industrial complex right in the face, and had to make a decision.

But...there is also a third way. To make a living out in regions like these, you don't necessarily have to settle for flipping burgers under the golden arches or engaging "terrorists" in whatever psy-op Uncle Sam and his greatest ally are cooking up at any given moment. Instead, if you keep your nose clean and stay out of trouble, you can do what I did. Go straight to jail.

I'm not talking about going to jail as a convicted felon, of course. What kind of dirtbag do you think I am? Instead, I'm speaking of a much darker fate: going to prison to earn your keep as a Corrections Officer.

All kidding aside, if you're willing to don the blue shirt and walk into the stinking maw of a concrete madhouse every day, the average person can stand to gain quite a bit. There's steady pay. Job security. A solid pension. Benefits (or "bennies" as some of us call them) and a daily respite from the old lady. It's a fantastic way for ordinary, rural, blue-collar Americans to latch onto a bit of material security in an age when everything, and I mean *everything*, seems completely uncertain, especially amid the rising fires of 2020 and beyond.

But, like most things in life, there's a catch. In exchange for stability, your average hack (jail-speak for officer) is going to suffer some seriously fucked up shit. Had I known back then what I know now, I would have looked at that state paycheck and tin (jail-speak for badge) a whole lot differently. Sure, it makes for a decent living, and most days end up pretty dull, but if you *do* decide to tread this path like countless others have before, remember one thing: they don't pay you to clock in and play cards.

They pay you for all those times you have to risk your life to control someone else. They pay you to endure nightmarish visions of a world turned upside down. They pay you to toil in service of chaotic policies that change at a whim. And they pay you to spend a full twenty-five years behind bars, eight hours at a time. For many, it's just honest work. For others, it's a waking nightmare.

From the first day you put on the badge until the day you turn it in, you serve as a jackboot for the Department of Corrections. No matter in which facility you punch your time-card, you serve as a state-sponsored mercenary, expected to work as a soulless, dour automaton without independent thought or feeling. You are loathed by the public you serve, despised by the inmates you watch, and taken for granted by the Department that signs your checks. The only people you can rely on during this service are your close family and the others who share your fate. We call them brothers. And sisters too. They are people from all walks of life who take up that heavy badge, clock in every day, and when you ask how they're doing, they will inevitably grin widely and reply that they're just "livin' the dream."

It's a dark reality, and whether as an inmate or as an officer, life behind bars can be a very scary place. But Hollywood's interpretation of prison life is a far cry from reality. Simultaneously, the government's rosy, orderly portrayal of County, State, and Federal Corrections is equally as ridiculous. With so few sources of accurate reporting, where can the average man access the truth about correctional life?

Right here.

This book lays it all on the table. Every hazard, every scenario, every insanity is presented the way it *actually* was, and is. No punches will be pulled, no quarter will be given, and, if you forgive the play on words, no prisoners will be taken.

I was a Corrections Officer for five years in the State of New York Department of Corrections and Community Supervision (or

NYSDOCCS for short), and while I may not have become the most senior officer, I certainly clocked enough hours to have seen some awful, eye-gouging shit. What you are about to read in these pages are real stories, experienced by real officers, which took place in real, honest-to-God correctional facilities. While I won't be using any real names for legal reasons, I guarantee the authenticity of every word herein.

So I ask you, dear reader, to sit back and prepare yourself for a grisly tour of life within the average correctional department. You're going to be offended; you're to be dumbfounded; you might even laugh *and* cry. But my only request is that you get righteously furious. It's going to be a hell of a ride. An education even. This is a crystal clear window into a world normally obscured. And it is dedicated to those who are just "livin' the dream."

Respectfully submitted,

C.O. Jack McKraken

1

NEW JACK CITY

*What to expect in Corrections Academy,
and how it's more "HR" than "PT"*

Have you seen the 1981 cult classic *Stripes*? It stars John Candy, Bill Murray, and the late, great Harold Ramis as they bumble their way through U.S. Army boot camp. Picture life at Corrections Academy as something similar, only twice as pathetic and thrice as tedious as the film itself (the second half anyway; the first half ruled).

For accepted correctional recruits, the Academy is where it all begins. For eight soul-sucking weeks, kids as young as twenty-one and geriatrics as old as Methuselah join together for push-ups, boot polishing parties, lousy chow, and about fourteen different classes detailing just how quickly you will be fired for racism. It has its ups, and it has its horrible, bottomless downs. But the biggest takeaway from Corrections Academy isn't any of the practical knowledge imparted. It is the iron truth that you can be held liable and then terminated for just about anything that might occur while you're on the clock at any time during your entire career.

And I mean *anything*.

An inmate isn't where he is supposed to be? You're done. You accidentally left a door unlocked in your area? Bye-bye! You inadvertently broke an arm in a ten-man fracas? Kiss that pension goodbye. One quickly transforms from a bright-eyed and bushy-tailed civilian, eager to serve the public in a law enforcement capacity, to nothing but a petrified wimp utterly subservient to bureaucratic policymakers AND the hardened criminals seething with rebellion. As it turns out, that's exactly how the State wants their correctional officers: aware of the rules, but too timid to uphold them. Ready and willing to jump into a fight if necessary, but too self-conscious and indecisive to use reasonable force when

8

necessary!

To appear politically correct before litigious metropolitan lawyers and radical leftist watchdogs like the ACLU and the SPLC, the State strategically inculcates beta-male attitudes into their recruits in an attempt to limit legal liabilities and prevent public relations disasters. Of course, anyone with an ounce of common sense realizes this makes for poor prison security. Yet this is the grim reality in which all correctional officers find themselves. If the watchman's hands are effectively tied, he is ultimately a gelding. Cucked. Charged with one of the most challenging responsibilities on earth, yet prevented from deploying the most effective methods.

This cruel double standard is not immediately apparent to the wide eyes of the correctional recruit, however. Instead, this sick ideology is slowly imprinted over eight weeks of training, and by the time you know the score, you're just about ready to graduate and receive orders to your first facility. It's death by slow boil. And it's so effective that some officers don't wake up to reality for years, if ever!

The State spends a lot of money to perfect this insidious kool-aid. And trust me, their formula is good.

When I first applied to be a CO, it was years before I got the call to enroll in the Academy proper. I had just about given up on the prospect altogether, and was a hair away from joining a more respectable outfit like the Navy. But the State came a-callin' and I was quick to answer, even if it was five years behind schedule.

So I showed up to do the bit: dolled up in an ill-fitting suit, waiting outside the very Academy that had nearly lost my interest. But it wasn't just me of course; there were dozens of us, of all shapes and sizes, ages, genders, and even nationalities. There was even a contingent of young recruits from the Virgin Islands shipped all the way to New York just for a chance at this hustle. I'm not sure what social program brought them there; it was probably some State attempt to flaunt its progressive, liberal values. Either way, I don't think many, if any, made it to graduation.

As we waited in line in front of the main building, a converted seminary that was as intimidating as it was beautiful, we were hit with the bracing air of a waning February. All of us shivered from the frigid winds stemming from the last gasps of winter around us, but also from anxiety. But as we waited to be processed and shown to our rooms, we quickly took notice of whole packs of drill instructors pacing up and down the line taunting, mocking, and intimidating those who were least-prepared. Luckily I managed to fly under the radar, but a poor twenty-something from Ithaca just a few places behind me got the scolding of a lifetime.

Apparently no one told him about the strict no-beards policy, and that all prospective recruits were to arrive cleanly shaven. As a result, two burly, red-faced drill instructors bellowed at him as if he had just shot their dogs. They called him names of every kind and demanded he address his "ZZ-Top costume. ASAP!"

So he did. Right there. Out in the upstate cold, with a cheap disposable razor that he nervously dug out from his suitcase. I don't know how he did it without any water or shaving cream, but the man somehow found a way.

"Sheesh," we all thought. We knew this wasn't going to be a walk in the park, but we did *not* expect a Parris Island vibe. Intense early moments like these set the tone for the rest of the Academy experience. And it worked...for a while.

After we signed our papers, found our rooms, and received our uniforms, we were ordered to square away our things and be ready for what lay in store for us early the next morning. That gave us precious little time to prepare ourselves. We had to make sure our uniforms were ironed, pants were hemmed, and lockers arranged in compliance with Academy directives. During this frenzied, late-night tornado of sweat and fatigue, we quickly learned to work together to get the job done. If one of us made a mistake, we realized we were all in trouble, and not just the offending dumbass who left a lousy crease in his shirt.

There were four of us to a room in the training academy, and in each room were two rickety bunk beds to split amongst ourselves. There I met my roommates, my brothers in arms for the next eight weeks. All in all, they were solid dudes. One of them, Martin, was an older guy in his fifties. He was more suited to be a used car salesman than a CO, but he was in the Army when he was younger, so he gave us tips when it came to making our bunks and checking off all the other "paramilitary" bullshit that the State demanded from us.

Then there was McNulty: a young, cocky guy who had a lot of energy and a positive attitude. There was Moreau, a slow-talking country kid who could not stop jabbering about hunting and trapping adventures back home. He was a little slow on the uptake, but would always offer to do our ironing because he had a real knack for military creases, and he legitimately enjoyed it for whatever reason.

Finally, there was Michel. He was one of the Virgin Island transplants. He had large, thick-rimmed eyeglasses and a deep voice coated in a Caribbean patois.

He was also about five hundred pounds.

When we first arrived, I made the dangerous mistake of picking a bottom bunk. I'm a pretty big dude myself and didn't feel comfortable risking life and limb on the top spot of a bunk bed built sometime at the beginning of the Cold War. No sooner did I choose when Michel ambled in, the last of us to arrive. He said his hellos, shook our hands, and quickly claimed the bunk directly above me. My eyes widened.

"Dude," I exclaimed. "It's cool; you can have my bunk."

But Michel, determined guy that he was, insisted I stay put. He didn't want to trouble me with having to switch spots. So off he climbed, reaching for the top bunk with belly exposed as he hauled his obese form up and over the top. The whole bed creaked and swayed. The other guys stayed quiet and smiled, knowing damn well it would end poorly for both of us if Michel destroyed state property on day one and killed me in the process.

I'll give him credit, though. It took him a few tries, but he finally made it on top. The springs above me worked like a champion that night, supporting Michel like the shoulders of Atlas. And thank God, too. I was beginning to wonder if this was the same level of fear that the COs at Attica felt during the 1971 riots. The next night Michel came to his senses, we switched beds, and life got a little easier for both of us.

In the morning they fed us, and I use the term lightly. Chow at Corrections Academy is somewhere between slop and dog food, just acceptable for human consumption and not much else. Later on, I came to realize that most of it was what they served inmates behind bars, only with slightly more variety and a boatload of condiments to mask the suck. So we did. Often.

There was also a never-ending jar of peanut butter on the chow line, just in case you got tired of eating whatever it was they were serving as the main course. By Graduation, I was practically living off the stuff, and it's a custom that followed me to this day.

One particularly nasty trap was the dessert window. A revolving display of treats near the end of the chow line filled with puddings, cakes, and other indulgences. Anyone could take one if they were so inclined, but God help you if a DI caught you anywhere near an empty calorie. You'd be doing "side-straddle hops" and "Jane Fondas" (a squat, push-up, then jumping-jacks) until you die.

One particular DI, a rodent of a man I'll call Derringer, relished in the pain of recruits. He was barely five-foot-five, sported a thick black mustache, and was the picture of a "Drill Instructor" as you might find one on the primetime television series *To Catch a Predator* with Chris Hansen. He would often accuse us of associating with the wrong women, and how ladies by the name of "Sara Lee," "Aunt Jemima," and "Little Debbie" were only there for our money and were going to make us soft.

Funny? Yes. But evil. Very evil. As it turns out, Drill Instructors at the Academy were no better or higher in rank than a run-of-the-mill officer. They were hacks just like me, or McNulty, or even Michel for that matter. They spent the greater part of the day examining us with a fine-tooth comb for the smallest Academy infractions, from laundry creases to dull boots, all while yelling the absurdities of the day at us. They made a lot of assumptions about our worth and carried on about how we would be no better than the old-timers and "soup-sandwiches" that worked in the prisons back home. But the only real difference between us and the DIs was that while we were preparing to go *into* the jails, they were up here hosting gym class and doing their best to stay *out* of them.

They weren't all bad guys, though. My particular DI was fairly typical. A few years later, rumors swirled that Derringer got caught sexually harassing female recruits. I guess in the end, it was HE who was associating with the wrong women.

Despite the sweat, the groans, and the short sleepless nights, the Academy tried its best to educate us in the most practical skills a CO needs to know on the job. Every week of Academy life was packed with tedious classwork and dedicated to specific subjects. One week taught you how to defend yourself; the next taught you relevant laws and regulations and how they applied to inmates. One week was dedicated to weapons, like how to "properly load and unload a department weapon," followed by range time and familiarity with the weapons themselves.

All these classes were taught by instructors, men and women who volunteered for recruit training in Albany and were selected in a murky, clandestine process that still eludes me. They were effectively leaving their home facilities for extended periods of time for a temporary home in Albany. They were trading their housing unit and yard bids for a cushy job at the front of a classroom, educating young recruits on how to be a CO, even though they were barely officers themselves. These instructors didn't make any extra money for their efforts, they rarely had seniority, and much like drill instructors, they too were the same rank-and-file officers we aspired to be upon graduation. What motivated them? Was instilling proper correctional values into young and eager ears their calling? Was teaching the proper way to handle a set of keys to newjacks the only way for them to get their rocks off? Or was it something else? Greed? Laziness? Cowardice?

Regardless of the motivations of our state-issued teachers, the classes themselves were typically boring and filled with heaps of bureaucratic minutia. I still can't remember a week that didn't end with a rundown of the answers that were going to appear on the upcoming test, usually held every Friday before you went home for the weekend. The rumor was that instructors had to show their value as teachers, and this value was reflected in the grades we received on our weekly exams. The higher our scores, the more likely our instructors would be retained for future classes. While it wasn't a particularly challenging curriculum, the classes *did* do exactly what they were designed for: to make the State as bulletproof as possible once we were put into action.

No courses revealed this blatant "cover your ass" ethos more than those on IPC, or Interpersonal Communications. These were a series of classes on how to speak with inmates in a correctional setting, or more accurately, how to not be a dickhead 101. I often wondered how much taxpayer money went into developing this farce, designed to humiliate white men and instill a sense of inferiority toward their captive wards. I also wondered if they instead used the money to pay us higher wages, would they get more compliant, less ornery employees overall? But what do I know? I'm just a hack.

What I know for sure is that the State's efforts to regulate human interaction as official policy is as ridiculous as it is ineffective. It boils down to this: when an inmate (i.e., a murderer or rapist) is escalating a situation, a CO is expected to de-escalate the situation. You're expected to ignore all the spitting, shouting, and calls to violence without so much as a blink. Prime examples of how to accomplish something like this include "taking a deep breath" and "engaging the inmate in distracting conversation" like, "Where are you from?"

"I understand your frustration."

"Ever been to a Bills game?"

This ill-conceived method of manipulating an angry person

during actual duress does not work. Trust me, we all tried. These are big, bad State prisons, not customer-service lines at Target.

To really hammer home this litigious liability bullshit, recruits at the Academy must undergo an inane "role play" session, in which senior officers don inmate outfits and enter a mock cell. They bully you, damage property, threaten injury, and a chosen recruit must calm the inmate and demonstrate to the rest of the class just how pathetic and sniveling he is by regurgitating the State's social dogmas.

Needless to say, our class failed the role-play session. We responded to the mock inmates too harshly, just like any sane person would react when threatened with the murder of their family back home. In practice, the State's "IPC" techniques were too awkward and too unrealistic to perform without hating yourself for even entertaining something so idiotic. Imagine telling a six-foot-five four-hundred-pound inmate that you feel his pain, and understand where he's coming from?

In clown world, you can. In reality, you can't. And that's because under no circumstance will a normal, well-adjusted human being ever want to help a mammoth felon with his lack of agency and rash decision making. You'll never know how he feels or really understand his situation, whether it's cultural or racial or economic underliers. It's just not going to happen. Still, the State expects you to try, and as a result, lie to their face. Lying and deceit are not western values, but to follow the State's idea of proper communication, one must violate those values. Lies and deceit toward an incarcerated individual to mask true intentions does not elevate one above the convict; if anything, it lowers one to their standards.

We'll get to *ideal* communication with inmates and how things *actually* work in the real world in later chapters. Use some creative license until then. But understand the complete insanities Corrections Officers are expected to adhere to on their first big-boy tours. It's dangerous, and not just for officers, but everyone involved.

Yet the danger doesn't stop at irresponsible policy! The second most ridiculous (but unquestionably most fun) aspect of corrections is the chemical weapons. Despite being banned by the Geneva Convention, State correctional departments and law enforcement agencies all over the United States and abroad *love* to deploy pepper spray and CS (tear) gas at the slightest provocation. And thank God they do! I have fond memories of playing with the State's vast collection of gases, sprays, and peppery perfumes. At Corrections Academy, recruits have to undergo a basic understanding of chemical weapons: what they look like, how to deploy them, and when/where it is acceptable to do so. During this education, a recruit quickly realizes just how much money is spent to keep the State's prisoners in line. From grenades to launchers to cluster bombs, the State arsenal is stuffed with just about every delivery system you can imagine. There's even a big machine called the "fogger" which produces CS gas in big puffy clouds, allowing you to bring down unholy discomfort on whole areas if you so desire. In the Academy, you get to play around with it a little bit, but not before you undergo a right-of-passage before graduation.

You have to get gassed.

Anyone reading this with a military or law enforcement background knows that exposure to chemical agents is required before they can be used on the job. Familiarization breeds competency or something. Regardless, before graduation we were lined up outside a rickety shack on an upstate mountain, shoved in with a bunch of other nervous recruits, and then gassed. We were supposed to stay in as long as possible, maybe answering a few questions from the mask-wearing DIs, but most cadets immediately ran straight out the door gasping for air. And that's what I did too. It felt like breathing in molten hot razor blades or crazed, flesh-eating fire-ants. It was a trip!

But in the Academy's twilight weeks, the focus shifted from physical training and practical usage to more "corporate" endeavors. We were still expected to commit to physical training from time to time, but things got a little different by week seven or eight. The pain of exercise didn't hurt anymore, we no longer cared about sleep, and the once-terrifying big DI became just a mean older brother: ornery, but endearing. He was just as willing to help and advise you in your future career as he was to make you drop down and bang out a quick twenty push-ups. In the end, the curriculum shifted toward sensitivity training: how not to be sexist, how not to be racist, and how not to curse in public. It was your standard, boilerplate, corporate propaganda. How much of it sticks is anyone's guess, but judging by how many F-bombs and hard-Rs are dropped during the average shift, it's safe to assume the training does little to nothing.

In fact, I know it does nothing.

During week eight, the whole session (or class, split into two groups labeled Alpha and Bravo) was excited for graduation. We had received our first assignments, pressed our class-A uniforms, and finally received our collar brass and badges from the higher-ups. Then one evening as we sat in the old chapel going over dress rehearsal for graduation ceremonies, a mean-mugged suit from the Inspector General's office walked in and demanded to see five guys from Alpha session.

Right away, it was clearly serious. DIs rarely look nervous, but in this moment they seemed absolutely petrified. The five named recruits were soon filed out of the chapel. It was the last time they sat with us together as brothers. Suddenly, they were gone, and I never saw them again. As confused as I was, the brothers and sisters in Alpha session, with whom they shared a class, were even more flabbergasted.

It turns out all of the recruits pulled out of the chapel that night were targeted. They were ratted out by a fellow recruit—one who, unbeknownst to us at the time, didn't particularly like several of his classmates. The snitch was a conniving black, a creature eager to leverage his racial power over unsuspecting white men by putting pen to paper anytime his targets used off-color language, cut a corner, discussed controversies, or anything that might be deemed inappropriate by the State's investigatory nannies. For weeks, this individual had been socking away information, and instead of meeting them face-to-face to air his grievances like a man, he sent his rat-log not to his DIs, not to the Sergeants, nor the Lieutenants, nor even the Captains!

He sent his journal directly to the Superintendent. The boss. The big man. All it takes is one bad incident to reach a Superintendent's ear, and it can mean the difference between a cushy career and a painful one. Superintendents (or sometimes more popularly referred to as Wardens) control *everything* in a correctional facility: how it's run, how it looks, and where the money is spent. And considering the inherently political nature of the job, it behooves Superintendents to keep their prisons as free from trouble as humanly possible.

The Academy is no different in this regard. If anything, the rules there are doubly stringent, and when you're a correctional recruit, your mandatory year-long probation hangs over your head like the Sword of Damocles. And that sword fell on the Alpha Five before they could even step foot in a prison. With no protections granted to them by the union, the State was able to terminate their careers before they even began. They were plucked like a dead flower out of a fresh bouquet all because one fellow black cadet cried racism.

Now, officers messing with each other during downtime is neither a rare nor new phenomenon. Busting balls is a ritual older than time itself. But if you're green, it's dangerous business unless you're one hundred percent confident the person in your sights is a friend. New guys live under a microscope, and if they so much as fart in the direction of a wrong individual, and they can stand to lose their career forever.

The whole incident went over as well as getting coal on Christmas. The news rocked the entire session. Five of our best guys, all strong, dedicated white men who did nothing but speak freely in private were escorted from the building, never to don the blue shirt again. While I never got the specifics, I did catch some gossip. Apparently some jokes were made, and the jokers had the unfortunate preexisting condition of being white in the presence of a black rat.

"Targeted because of his race," claimed the informant. "Too bad," we all thought. But at least now for the rest of this guy's career, he would to be targeted for being something else: a snitch.

Graduation loomed regardless, and preparations accelerated. The DIs had us marching in formation, shining our boots, and informing us of what it was *really* like to be a CO once we reached our first facilities. We took everything they told us with a grain of salt. The shiny, gilded veneer of life as a New York State Corrections Officer was already beginning to crack, and we hadn't even graduated yet.

During that final week, aside from keeping our noses clean long enough to stay employed, we had to draft a graduation speech and elect who among us would deliver it during the ceremony. The only problem was that after the dark drama in Alpha Session, no one wanted to. A silent protest was spreading through the ranks. No one felt the pride or optimism to be the guy or girl on stage in front of all the staff and families to extol the Department of Corrections' values and virtues. We were still furious, and rightfully so. To read a gung-ho speech after knowing what we knew just felt wrong.

At some point the DIs caught wind of our little insurrection and stamped it out promptly. A whole graduating class rejecting the traditions of an overtly weak system was not going to be tolerated. Since we were still soft and impressionable, the entire movement collapsed. The DIs weren't hard on us, though, and I sensed sympathy from them for the very first time. Despite their hard exterior and expertly-pressed uniforms, they spoke to us not as Drills, but as brothers—fellow Corrections Officers who felt just as resentful and remorseful as we were.

Their honesty won us over more than their direct orders to, "cut the shit."

A short, skinny, Hispanic kid named Julian eventually agreed to recite the speech. Our squad leader (a clean-cut country boy and ex-jarhead) opted to write it, but because he was more bone than brain, the duty fell on me.

Everything went off without a hitch. A couple hours of pomp and circumstance later, we all finally held our diplomas and badges. As the crowd applauded and our families and friends gathered to watch us march proudly into a new career, it felt good. We were finally through with the Academy and could now start working full-time in a real-life jail. But while my head was high with accomplishment, a pit in my stomach grew. What exactly did I learn here? If I showed up to work tomorrow, was I prepared for the worst? Was I even prepared for the best?

Uncertainty took root within our hearts as we left the Academy that day, and we planned to never to return to it again. We had just spent eight weeks learning "how to be a Corrections Officer," and when we tried to go over all we were taught by the State, we struggled to even describe the things we learned. Certainly there was new legal knowledge in there. We also knew to avoid the word, "Nigger." And handcuffing? We spent about half an hour on handcuffing.

We were marching into our first posts stronger and less likely to be State liabilities. But we were just as green and useless as jailers as when we first arrived. For us, the real training was about to begin. The whole Academy experience, from start to finish, had a lingering stench about it. And that stench never went away.

* * *

This chapter is dedicated to the five white men of Alpha session. If you're reading this, you know who you are. You were robbed of your careers before they began, not just by a lone rat gunning for a civil suit, but also by the ineffectual, leftist policies adopted by the New York State Department of Corrections and Community Supervision. You may have forgiven or even forgotten about the injustices by now, but *I am still mad for you.* You were professionally crucified for your race, and you deserve a voice. I hope mine does yours service.

2

BANGING-IN

*Skirting responsibility and how every
party is guilty of passing the buck*

When I was a kid, I'd often hear my dad complain about work while he drained a six-pack or two. "Johnny," he'd say, "I'm not going to work. It's glorious outside. I think I'm going to bang-in." It was a strange, almost dirty term to hear coming from an adult, but I quickly learned to accept it for what it was: a blue-collar way to say "staying home."

Fast forward a few decades later and there I was, all grown up and following in the footsteps of dear old dad: picking up the phone and "banging-in" like the best of them.

Don't get me wrong, I'm not wracked with guilt for indulging in a practice as old as time itself. We've all done it at some point in our lives (some more than others). But in a Correctional setting, "banging-in" can be an art form, and believe it or not, there's a lot that goes into skirting responsibility in this setting. In fact, it's the foundation of the Corrections profession.

And that's what this chapter is all about: skirting responsibility. CO's do it, inmates do it, even supervisors do it (and boy do they do it). But *how* one skirts responsibility differs depending on the individuals and the circumstances, and if you step back to see the bigger picture, it can even define the ethos of a prison as a whole.

The easiest way to get out of work is by banging-in. COs do this by calling their facility and informing their Chart Sergeants that they have a bad case of anal glaucoma (symptoms may include: not seeing your ass going to work today). The average officer then supplies some negligible information, the Sergeant records it, the timekeepers deduct some sick-time accruals, and *voila*, you're off to the track. The whole process is relatively painless, and most Sergeants are pretty cool with it. Hell, they do the same when they don't want to come in either. The only exception is when a hectic day is planned or if enough COs have already banged in. At that point, the Sergeant has to do the extra work of paying overtime to cover the shirkers. "Filling holes," they call it, and it must not be fun. I've seen six-foot-tall, three-hundred-pound men sweat bullets and turn redder than a baboon's ass when assigned this duty, and I always tried to leave the office before that stress lashed out at me.

But while calling out of work provides a great reprieve from the concrete hellscape for a day or two at most, the suffering doesn't just vanish altogether. No, much like energy (which is neither created nor destroyed, as we learned in high school physics), the torment is instead transferred to another hapless officer. This is known as, "getting stuck." And it's one of the worst things that can ever happen in corrections, that is, save for maybe catching herpes from a prison toilet seat.

See, if you bang-in and there are no extras in the jail, and if there aren't not enough names on the overtime list, then the Sergeant has to begin "sticking" people already at work and assign them mandatory overtime.

So picture this: you started the day at 7 am and woke up at 5 am to arrive on time. You're tired, you're hungry, and you told the old lady you'd pick up Little Caesar's on the way home for dinner because you found a coupon in the penny-saver. Suddenly, it's 2:45 pm, only fifteen minutes left, and you're almost free of this woeful place. But then, just as you were about to zip up your state-issued clear lunch bag and head to clock out, you get called on the radio by "Command." Shit! Your heart sinks to your bowels, and your very soul drains away. You are stuck again.

Typically, this means you'll work a double-shift with no advance notice. Sixteen hours of correctional responsibility, with only a quick six-hour nap before your next shift the following day. It's a fate that no CO seeks, yet it's a fate that no CO can avoid forever. Depending on the jail, your average hack can be stuck in this quagmire dozens of times a year, and sometimes multiple times a week!

Another way to get out of work without killing sick time is to swap. Swapping is great because it gives you plenty of time to plan your days off in advance; it just requires is a little diplomacy and a stooge willing to come in to work in your place. The catch, of course, is that you'll have to go in and become the new stooge at some point in the near future. (Remember that energy cannot be destroyed?

That applies here as well). As long as you plan carefully, swaps can be an integral part of your career. Some CO's manage to find partners to swap with regularly for years at a time. Instead of coming in to work a full week, some manage to game the swap system in a way, so that they only work two double-shifts in a row and then enjoy a whopping four days off. It sounds great on paper, but in practice, it can be a complete nightmare. Some people love it; I never figured it out personally, but more power to 'em. They say it takes a special kind of person to work corrections (see: mentally unhinged and low IQ), but it takes an extra special kind of person to be a serial swapper (deranged and masochistic).

But for those not into the swapping scene, there's still plenty of ways to get time off. On top of sick time and swaps, CO's are also allowed a set amount of vacation time that they accrue throughout the year. You can spend this time by "dropping slips" on days you might need off, or by bidding on set vacation slots at the start of every year. Overall, there's a lot of flexibility with the amount of time you can take off. The same goes for your work schedule.

There's only one issue. In order for your time off to be approved, you have to go up against every CO who might want that day off too. The New York State Department of Corrections and Community Supervision settles these little disputes through the time-tested tradition of seniority.

Now, most Civil Service organizations operate on the system of seniority: police, firemen, mailmen...bureaucrats of all stripes. It's a blind kind of justice that rewards loyalty and time served (!) in the workplace above all else. It benefits older, saltier employees over the younger, greener ones. In the land of Corrections, everything from job bids, vacations, overtime, facility transfers, and even promotions are all based on seniority. This makes life a lot easier for old-timers but a living hell for new-jacks. If you're a new guy, chances are you won't get any decent days off in the summer or any good vacation weeks. Chances are you'll never get a holiday off. That cushy job in the tower? It's just not going to happen unless you get some serious time under your belt.

In NYSDOCCS, they often say, "time sucks until you got it." It's one of those sayings you hear repeatedly throughout your career, and you don't believe a word of it until it affects you personally. Once I had my eyes on a nice new bid in the yard: it wasn't tough duty, but not the best either. If I won that bid, I'd be able to enjoy the same position in the jail until I voluntarily gave it up for a different one,

JACK McKRAKEN

be it in a month or until I retired. Naturally, a guy who had just one week of seniority on me got that gig—one that might have even extended my life expectancy. "Oh well." I thought. "Better luck next time."

Your standard run-of-the-mill hack has many ways he can sidestep his duties, and we only covered the legal, official ways to do it thus far. If we dig a little deeper, we might uncover certain *other* methods to get out of doing a hard day's work. Methods such as finding a nice quiet out-of-the-way office somewhere and catching a few Z's. Or perhaps you could butter up some of the Sergeants and watch TV with them up in the Arsenal. Or, if you're feeling particularly bold, you could always leave your post and hang with your buddies in a completely different housing unit. I could write a whole book on how CO's game the system for a comfortable night, but to do so would omit so many other more egregious scams run by other prison personnel! Our green-shirted counterparts, the inmates, carry out most of them, but a fair deal of these sloth operations come from our white-shirted and suit-wearing supervisors as well.

I understand why a middle-aged, blue-collar hack working his second double in a row might seek to "rec out" for an hour in the back office, and I might be able to rationalize why a double-digit IQ inmate would skip out on his GED classes in favor of jerking-off and eating zippy cakes. But when it comes to Supervisors, I have nothing but contempt for their methods of avoiding labor. Nothing made my blood boil more than seeing or hearing a member of our esteemed leadership do *nothing* when they should have done *something*.

That boil would turn into a veritable conflagration when something terrible happened as a result of leadership lassitude. In Corrections, your decisions and actions always speak louder than your words. Talk is cheap, and sometimes you need a supervisor's backing to give your actions the weight they need to be taken seriously by an inmate that calls your bluff. If you're lucky, Sergeants, Lieutenants, and higher ranking officers will have your back if something goes wrong with an inmate. But covering our ass usually means extra work for the supervisor in question. They might have to relocate an inmate; maybe they'll have to file paperwork or complete some other bureaucratic inconvenience. Sometimes, that inconvenience can be so great that the supervisor will instead choose not to be inconvenienced. And if he does nothing, he leaves you vulnerable against a unit full of inmates that now know you're

23

more bark than bite.

The best ways I can explain this phenomenon is by this brief story. One time in the middle of summer, the sweltering heat hit the prison like a magnifying glass trained on a hapless ant. At the time, my partner, a portly but wise Irish guy with more time than God, received a snitch note from another inmate about drugs one inmate was peddling to the rest of the unit. My partner, let's call him Cagney, said we should go in to search the suspect's cell. The inmate in question was a particularly nasty one, an up-and-coming Blood who caused a lot of issues on the block. If we could go in there before the drugs were moved, and find and secure them as evidence, we could get him on a significant contraband charge and maybe even transferred out of the jail altogether.

Now, searching a hot, humid cell in a polyester state uniform with the sun beating onto your back was not exactly at the top of my list of priorities that day. But I had a lot of respect for Cagney and a lot of hate for that particular inmate.

So in we went. Sweat dripped from our brows the second we stepped inside the 6x10 tomb. We "flipped" the cell from top to bottom, going through every porno, every picture from home, every cassette tape, and every can of instant coffee. We checked the bedding, the walls, the lockers: anywhere a crafty convict might hide a bag of hard drugs, we searched. Just when it seemed like this was all for nothing, I looked at Cagney with eyes that stung from sweat.

"Nothin'," I said, my whole body feeling submerged. I had just upended an entire bin of zippy cakes onto the mattress and rifled through the pile.

"Look at this," Cagney mumbled.

In his hands lay a small cardboard box filled with packets of artificial sweeteners the convict had accumulated from the mess hall. He had it stashed behind the sink, an odd place for condiments to be sure. In the box amidst the usual contents, rest a small baggie filled with what looked like black crusty pebbles. Flakes, almost.

"What's that?" I asked.

Cagney smirked with his chubby Irish cheeks and glanced at me in his usual sly demeanor. "Black tar. Heroin," he replied.

That discovery made flipping a cell in 90-degree heat worth it. I had never seen drugs like that up close at the time, so our little sting made me feel pretty important, like a big shot detective on a hard case!

We took the heroin back to the bubble. This was a secure area where we could do our paperwork and observe the inmates at the same time. So far, everything pointed to a slam dunk case: We got the evidence, and the snitch note gave us probable cause. What could go wrong? All we had to do was pass the info and the drugs up the chain of command and...

"Flush it."

"What?!" asked Cagney. "Dave, we got him red-handed here. This will put him away in SHU."

"Really? A little bit of H? I thought you guys were real COs."

"But Dave, this guy is a real piece of shit, let's get him off the unit."

"Flush it," the Sergeant spat, his face growing a shade of red nearing purple. "The only thing I don't want on my unit is that."

Then, the Sergeant left the bubble, and as soon as he was out of earshot, the expletives flew.

"What a fat fucking slug," we both said, albeit in different varieties of obscenity. "That guy never had either of our backs."

Cagney went over to the toilet, which was wedged into a small closet in the bubble, dropped the heroin into the bowl, and flushed the first real piece of prison contraband I had ever seen into the public sewer system. At the time of that incident, I was still a young officer, the intoxicating highs of "Academy values" still lingering, like a latent but fading pride. But to see all that unfold before my eyes was a betrayal of the highest order. It felt dirty. Pathetic. And in that moment, those Academy values officially died for good.

During my career in DOCCS, there were many instances just like that one, and they happened on a fairly regular basis. Stories of officers getting their toes stepped on by cowardly bosses or a frightened administrator were regular occurrences, and my view of the Correctional system never improved. Guys like Cagney had years, even decades on the job, so these instances of professional incompetence had already taken its toll on them long ago. All that was left were men who had just enough resistance to mumble about the injustices but too compliant to fight.

But the real question is, why? Why did that particular Sergeant order us to throw out hard evidence, especially since it could send a rotten egg someplace far away to incubate? Why did he turn down a prime opportunity to stem the flow of a growing drug epidemic in the prison community as a whole, and potentially save lives?

Simple. That supervisor didn't want to do the work.

Normally in a situation like that, each officer involved would have to write a detailed report to the Sergeant. Then the evidence would have to be painstakingly secured by that Sergeant and properly inventoried. Then the officer who found the drugs would have to write a disciplinary ticket that would charge the inmate. And the Sergeant would have to file his own report comprised of all the other accumulated paperwork, ensure it was all in line, and deliver it to the Lieutenant for approval. Lastly, the Sergeant would assemble a team of men and escort the offending inmate to SHU (or Special Housing Unit) if appropriate.

Cognizant of all that, the Sergeant could fulfill his expected duties and do his job. Or he could just order the evidence flushed down the liquid waste memory hole. He could then return to his air-conditioned office and sleep. Or eat. Or watch TV. Or any other priorities he opted for instead.

That day, Sergeant Dave chose the latter, putting hardworking officers in an infuriating situation. What could have been a perfectly-executed bust of a known gang leader and drug-peddler living within the general population (and which would have interrupted drugs and violence wholesale throughout the prison, not to mention possibly saved a few inmates' lives) he chose the lazy option. If there's one thing I learned about NYSDOCCS during my time in its concrete caverns, it's that inaction harms both the prisoners and the guards far more than action does.

Look at it this way. Despite the constant smears of the Department by the media machine, the system is designed for a single purpose: to correct the behaviors of the incarcerated in a fair, firm, and consistent manner. It exists so that average law-abiding citizens can live in relative peace and safety, and so offenders can re-enter society as productive citizens after serving their sentences. But it *is* a system—a machine. For it to work as intended, every part needs to be working in coordination, or it will barely function at all. You can't drive a car without a transmission. You can't fly a plane without wings. And you can't have a functioning corrections system with a culture of sloth and shirking.

Yet that is exactly what we have: elite politicians and their appointed underlings running Correctional Departments across the country that amount to a broken machine. They never hesitate to tinker with the rules, policies, and specifics of the machine in the service of progressive interests. And none of it matters so long as the poison of skirting responsibility flows in the veins of the Correctional body.

Whenever a new liberal prison policy comes into effect, or an inmate walks free on a technicality, or a wrist is impotently slapped, or a violent youth offender is given a basketball instead of a beating: It's not because the state cares about anyone's well-being. It is because leadership *caved* to the demands of "polite" society and the temptation of easy choices. They apply another coat of paint onto a rusted old jalopy. And while they might be able to keep the bucket of bolts on the road for a little while longer, eventually, the whole damn thing will break down and become just another derelict on the side of the American freeway.

For things to work properly in the correctional system, principled action is always a requirement. I've borne witness to heaps of miserable middle management, and I've even seen my fair share of rather *good* middle management. But you have to understand: the kind of unforgivable indolence I witnessed that hot summer day with Sergeant Dave and Officer Cagney runs straight to the top of the Correctional hierarchy.

Even dutiful middle-management types, ones who are expected to lead and make good decisions, also get shafted for their efforts! I've seen great Sergeants try to make a difference, only to be blocked by their superiors at every turn. Autonomy in NYSDOCCS is not only discouraged but punished! Any initiative by an officer or supervisor puts him in the sights of more powerful men, and absent the most skilled implementation, results in getting chewed out, or "having your pee-pee slapped," as we say. I can't count the number of times a Lieutenant refused to allow an inmate to be locked up because it would ruin his quiet night, or how many really messed up situations were covered up or silenced just to prevent a "UI" or "unusual incident."

An "unusual incident" describes an atypical jailhouse event. Fights, assaults, contraband, riots, escapes, accidents: all of these are UIs, and Lieutenants and above are responsible for their reporting and management. They result in a ridiculous amount of work for an officer to prepare for his bosses, and each UI is a blemish against the facility in which it occurred. After too many UIs, a prison develops a reputation among the Albany elite as being a poorly-run circus. This then reflects badly on a Superintendent, who often has political aspirations of his own. It thus behooves these bosses to keep their jails as quiet and orderly as possible, even if that means sweeping disorder under the rug to game the statistics on quarterly reports and thus maintain "accreditation."

But how do you maintain order in an increasingly chaotic country? America's prison population is a veritable army of hardened criminals, most of whom are fighting-aged males with drug addictions and no real loyalty to Western society—and they are becoming harder and harder to contain. This issue is only exacerbated when you have politicians from both ends of the left-right dialectic coming out in support of inmates over the health and well-being of society. Take Jared Kushner, for example. While he may have served as senior advisor to Republican President Donald J. Trump, his pet project, the "First Step Act," would place him squarely in the same socialist camp that his father-in-law supposedly opposes tooth-and-nail. The act itself reduces the sentence time of federal inmates (especially drug-offenders), provides time credits towards pre-release custody programs, and even holds inmates by the hand and assists them in "applying for federal and state benefits and obtain identification, including a social security card, driver's license or other official photo identification, and birth certificate.[1]" While these efforts might be done in the name of recidivism among those individual inmates who are lucky enough to benefit, it does nothing to spurn the criminality that spawned the inmate to begin with. If anything, it expands it!

And this is coming from a Republican! If both sides of the political play-pen have decided that the lives of inmates far exceed the needs of a society still healing from their crimes, then who can the working man turn to for a solution? As it stands, all the concrete, assault rifles, barbed-wire and handcuffs in the world won't stop things like UIs from proliferating, or stop revolving-door prisons from revolving. So, a Superintendent's best weapon in this war of attrition is to simply cook the books and keep mum.

For example, one time a fellow officer of mine was threatened by a convict. The individual was a scumbag serving a life sentence for some terrible barbarity that would make your skin crawl. Upset over getting caught breaking a rule and catching a minor infraction, he threatened the officer's family on the outside. The rules dictate that inmates who make such threats be sent immediately to SHU for closer supervision and possible transfer to a different facility.

Yet in this case, leadership decided to "council and reprimand"

[1]Kushner, Jared. "Jared Kushner: What I've Learned From Criminal Justice Reform." *Time*, Time, 24 Apr. 2019, time.com/5577434/jared-kushner-criminal-justice-reform-lessons/.

the convict, while the full force of their wrath instead came down on that officer, who was pressured to shut up about the inmate's "empty threats." Empty? Could a high-ranking gang member and convicted killer with connections on the outside *maybe* use his resources to attempt a hit on that officer or his family? There are far too many people in NYSDOCCS and correctional departments across the country who allow this kind of behavior to thrive. It's endemic, and in some cases it's almost demanded of you. It's an outrage that needs to end.

But what can we expect from organizations like NYSDOCCS? It's an institution run for years by an "Acting Commissioner" because that maximizes pay and minimizes responsibility. The culture of running from responsibility is so strong that even people expressly in charge of the department openly flaunt their dereliction. It would infuriate an informed public, as it results in trickle-down lawlessness that eventually seeps out into our streets.

Yet here we are. As America reels from explosive growth in violent crime and social unrest, our prisons become weaker and more complacent. With every guard, supervisor, and department apparatchik avoiding action like the plague, how can Americans expect justice to ever be carried out, even when the bad guys get put away?

Absent severe top-down reform (which will be addressed in Chapter 17), it will never happen. Instead, line staff, civilians, inmates, and anyone else in the system will remain perilously perched atop a powder keg just awaiting a spark. Departments across the country must rid themselves of their top-down culture of "banging-in," or else we're all looking down the barrel of a loaded gun.

3

CONTRABAND

How banned items can get you jammed
up whether you're green, blue, or white

"He can't have that! That's contraband!" Officer Van der Berg wrinkled her nose and placed her hands on her hips in an exaggerated way. She stared at me with inquisitive eyes, waiting for me to make the next move. The next *correct* move, that is.

In my gloved hands rested an old, plastic Dunkin' Donuts travel mug. I had pulled it out of a convict's cell during a routine search. The inmate in question was an older man, and his Departmental Identification Number (DIN) indicated he had been in the system for a few decades already. He wasn't using the mug to hold liquids; instead, he found it useful for storing pens, pencils, and other knick-knacks in his cell. Upon Van der Berg's urging, those same contents now lay strewn upon his state-issued mattress, and the mug was now in my possession.

"Really?" I asked, half-confused and half-offended by the seemingly petty flex.

"Really," she shot back. "It's right here in the inmate handbook. Page 12, section sixty-nine. No containers or mugs over 32 ounces! Look at this thing; it's clearly 64 ounces!"

I took another look at it. Yeah, it was a little big for a mug, but so what? The thing was ancient. We're talking "time to make the donuts" old. Was I really the first CO to ever notice this super dangerous, highly illegal piece of contraband during this inmate's extended correctional stay? I hope not.

"Okay, so now what?" I asked. I was still a new officer at the time, and the finer details of contraband procedure were still daunting. There were lots of items on the list, and so far, it seemed like the average Correctional Officer ignored almost half of it.

"So now we'll have to leave it here in the bubble and secure it while you write out a Contraband Receipt and hand it over to the inmate."

"Okay."

So I did. I placed the old, crusty Dunkin' Donuts mug in the small officer's window of the bubble and did some quick paperwork. A part of me felt slimy for taking an old man's pencil box, but rules are rules. Van der Berg, degrading harpy that she was, stood before me looking thrilled to be teaching *the right way to do things.* Legally, I was doing nothing wrong. Morally, on the other hand...

"Here," I said, my arm outstretched through the bars, giving the inmate in question his copy of the contraband receipt I had filled out with a blue pen. "You're good on the search. But I took the mug. You can't have it."

"My mug? Really?" he asked.

"Yep."

"Why?" he asked, this time after sucking hard on his gapped front teeth.

"It's too big. It can't be over 32 ounces."

"Sheeeiiiit," he said sullenly. "I had that mug over twenny years. Ain't no CO ever said nothin' about it before!"

Now, most COs understand that cons will say just about anything to get their way—and I'm no con-lover, believe me. But the way he looked and the way he spoke told me all I needed to know. This guy was telling the truth.

I gritted my teeth and looked back at the bubble. Van der Berg stood there watching and waiting for me to make the correct move once again.

"Sorry, I don't make the rules," I said. The inmate took the receipt, and I walked away. He was a New York state inmate doing hard time in the pen, and somehow, I was the one feeling guilty!

In corrections, stories like this happen every day. Contraband, as the State defines it, is "any item that threatens the security of inmates, employees, visitors, and the community, and impairs rehabilitation programs." Common sense would define this as drugs, booze, weapons, or currency. But as it stands, items like over-sized coffee mugs and raw meat fall under that umbrella too. Contraband is a big, vague, gray-area, and inmates can easily find themselves inside that gray-area, depending on the CO working any given day.

Interestingly enough, the same applies to employees walking through the front gates. While I wouldn't want a co-worker to bring in dangerous items for the convicts, innocent officers do get jammed up or even fired for accidentally bringing a newspaper, book, or cell phone inside by mistake. What the State considers contraband is such a broad, all-encompassing net that innocent officers do get caught and dragged down with the rest of the less-innocent fish. It happens all the time.

Management cracks down on such contraband (especially the more dangerous stuff that gets smuggled into its facilities from outside) via extensive bag and body checks of everyone who enters a prison. The process is invasive and embarrassing, and it makes for an uneasy environment that widens the gap of mistrust between officers and their managers. Imagine your pencil-pushing boss, who is always bothering you at the water cooler, suddenly has the power to stop-and-frisk you? That's Corrections. What results is a workplace where Officers watch the cons, Management watches the Officers, the Governor and his cronies watch the Management. And the Cons? They watch everyone.

Still, contraband can be a useful tool for cons when used intelligently. Knowing which individual has access to what item and where it might be stashed can be quite the commodity for an enterprising inmate. Uncovering a stash can also make an ambitious employee look like a million bucks to his supervisors. It wasn't uncommon for Sergeants and above to make power plays on a housing unit by searching cells and common areas, all so that they could find some weak sauce contraband and be the talk of the line-up room the next morning. Whether management entertained these transparent gambits always depended on the individuals involved, but these petty searches happened quite a bit.

Once during the cooler months of autumn, and as the big yard was on the go-back (prison speech for returning from outdoors and into the housing unit), one convict was chosen for a random search. Within a secret pocket sewn into his state-issued pants was a small baggie of weed. Not long after, the inmate was cuffed and taken to SHU per protocol.

At this inmate's disciplinary hearing, he cut a deal with the Lieutenant in charge for a lighter sentence. Essentially, he ratted out a slew of his fellow inmates, and it worked out pretty well. For us.

Four knives, as long as roman short-swords, were soon discovered in the carpentry shop, stashed away in secret for just the right time. "CO killers," he called them. Their removal made us all feel safer, but it also served the dual purpose of reminding us just how dangerous our workplace could be.

By the end of the day, the Executive team extolled its policies, management barely acknowledged our efforts, but we all felt great for nabbing some serious cutlery. In reality, if that convict hadn't remembered where those weapons were and gave them up in a self-serving deed, they would have remained available for murder. Instead, he used their existence as currency and spent it wisely: he won reduced SHU time and a transfer shortly after. A win-win scenario.

This reveals why contraband in a prison setting is so valuable. Whether or not an item is ever used, there are a thousand ways it can be bartered for something else entirely. In the eyes of an inmate, a bag of heroin could just be a means to get high. Or it could look like currency, ready to be traded for something else at a second's notice without a CO ever noticing the exchange. And this is usually done by passing contraband through willing (and sometimes unwilling) inmates who get a cut of the action themselves.

Due to strict policies on the cleanliness of areas like corridors and housing units, inmate porters, janitors, handymen, and other cons working the unit are often tasked by peers to traffic contraband from one cell to another. Porters are typically out with a broom or mop in hand, scrubbing floors and windows during periods of downtime in the jail. This is a brief time during the day when all other inmates are locked in their cells or otherwise confined, and when CO's can finally get a minute to relax. But as the porter cleans the unit, other inmates will leave items on the bars of their cell so they can be passed around the gallery. When a porter picks an item up, the convict behind bars will shout to the porter where it's going. Then, using his temporary freedom to wander the gallery, the porter drops it off on the bars of the receiving inmate. He is the inmate mailman, and will keep performing this vital service until everyone's trades are fulfilled. Once finished, he locks himself back up, usually when his porter responsibilities are up or when he gets caught red-handed by a C.O.

Now, the porter doesn't do this out of the kindness of his heart. For his troubles come obvious risks, but those risks are rewarded in the form of compensation from other inmates. He can expect to see a small cut, usually cakes, cigarettes, or anything inmates might have on hand to use as a tip. Porters get a little richer by the end of the day, and the riches keep coming as long as they remain in the game. This makes the porter's job on a housing unit a lucrative one, with some inmates competing with others to see who can fill the role and reap the rewards. But there's a catch. You have to be good at it. Bad porters will be spotted a mile away by security staff, ending their hustle quickly. The job also requires finesse, and the ability to schmooze without drawing too much attention to yourself. It also requires someone who actually knows how to clean. If a porter is terrible at his primary function (i.e., mopping and sweeping), he can get summarily fired by a CO. I know this because I did it myself numerous times.

If a unit is in real horrible shape, sometimes the gangs will flex on the rest of the unit to ensure only their guys get porter gigs. Intra-gang trades get priority; everyone else's mail effectively goes undelivered. Powerful gangs like the Bloods or Latin Kings can completely dominate a unit's economy in this way, and if an inmate is not in good graces with the brothers running things, he won't be getting anything passed. He won't be getting on the phone anytime soon, either.

Alternatively, the porter role can sometimes fall to a weak or desperate inmate. This is a unique situation. In this case, the porter might do the job for free, passing just about anything to anyone out of fear instead of avarice. Addicts are a particularly bad choice for this job, however, as they're always tempted to skim off any narcotics deliveries.

This process continues, day in and day out. Regardless of how contraband enters a facility, it always finds a means of travel once inside. Even if an officer on duty decides to tail a porter to make sure there are no shenanigans, the entire unit will wait for him to turn his back or sit back down, and then business resumes. If that isn't an option, inmates will simply put their game on hold long enough for an officer to clock out, and happily see the job done once the next hack clocks in.

Minor contraband discoveries usually result in disciplinary charges for the possessor. Inmates receive slaps on the wrist for breaking these codes, and at most see their goodies taken out of circulation and some sort of recreation denied for his transgression. Simply put, there's no real deterrence for smuggling or holding any of these banned items. Contraband policy does little to impede the behavior, other than placing a speed bump in front of an inmate's larger criminal tendencies. If it's not drugs or weapons, it's almost not even worth it for a CO to enforce contraband rules. Overeager enforcement earns laughs from the supervisors who approve disciplinary tickets.

NYSDOCCS contraband policy is more often a hammer used against its own employees than it is against the inmates it claims to correct. The number of hoops a Correctional Officer jumps through just to work an honest eight-hour shift is hugely demoralizing. Before entering the average facility, an officer is subject to a bag check, a pat-down, a metal detector scan, and searches of lockers and work areas at any given moment. If caught with anything at all, even something that another officer may have left behind, expect harsh discipline and even non-paid leave until the Department figures out what to do. It's a life lived in utter fear that at any time, a boss or outside agency can fleece you, and if you refuse to submit, receive immediate suspension for your principles. Contraband policy is worse on officers than it is on inmates. Officers cannot stop their bodies from being violated by a pair of gloved hands at any moment, and have even less power to wiggle their way out of trouble if it arises.

That lunchmeat in your bag? It better be fully cooked, because if not, that's contraband. The pens you brought in to write reports and document inmates on the go-around? They better be fewer than the state limit. The same goes for your cigarettes, eyeglasses, and the cash in your wallet. Every item on your person can be scrutinized by the bureaucratic microscope. And if the local administration isn't particularly fond of you, they can leverage these purposefully vague rules against you. Which of course can easily result in disciplinary measures up to and including termination.

Prisons will often conduct major searches; these are supposedly random, but always end up being time-consuming and all-encompassing. Whenever these occurred in the facilities I worked, the brass would stand out near the front gates and during shift change, would scan every CO's inventory and personal items for contraband. Anyone found with anything remotely questionable, like a lukewarm burger or, God forbid, a cellphone, would receive quick and merciless disciplinary action.

But special exemptions were sometimes provided for the day shift. Unlike the evening and midnight shifts, the day-timers might see a big garbage can left outside just before the line started, allowing employees to dispose of newspapers, books, Sudoku puzzles, and anything close to risky. This allowed them to ditch stuff before they were searched, allowing for a clean, easy operation and a hassle-free report to the brass. My shift was never afforded this luxury. As a CO I worked evenings, and we always seemed to be the guinea pigs for big searches like these. The same could be said for midnight shifts. We were always hammered hardest by the administration when it came to arbitrary, random pushes for prison compliance, and it built animosity between the tours.

Why does this happen? I couldn't give you a straight answer. Maybe it was because the guys on day shift tended to be older, more senior officers, and the administration wanted to cut them a break. Maybe the Captain and Lieutenants in charge of the day search just wanted a flawless operation and were just "banging-in" on that responsibility. Whatever the reason, the injustice of the entire practice was revolting. In Corrections, one of the big concepts emphasized is always treating others in a firm, fair, and consistent manner above all else. When it came to the Department's policy on contraband and its searches, that firm, fair, and consistent principle was all but a lie.

In the Corrections world, the inmate fears the CO, the CO fears the brass, and the brass fears the Governor's office or any muckraking NGO that might dip its beak into the facility like it was a fresh charcuterie board. The Correctional structure, from the bottom up, is entirely run and maintained by omnipresent fear. And maintaining that fear is paramount to the everyday operations of the Department. Without it, the shaky house of cards falls apart.

Now, don't get me wrong. Any facility employee caught doing something inexcusable like smuggling drugs or weapons into the jail should lose his career. Betrayal of the public trust and jeopardizing prison safety deserves banishment. But when good guys fall under the sights of brutal, heavy-handed Departmental policies while inmates get their wrists slapped, it makes you want to scream. During my career in the system, I've seen plenty of innocent men and women get in trouble for absolutely nothing. Literally nothing. And why? Because the Machiavellian contraband policy that is selectively enforced creates an utterly lopsided power dynamic. While inmates might be the intended target, Correctional Officers are far too often collateral damage.

Good men are punished for having *Hydroxycut.*

Good men are punished over *lunchmeat.*

Good men are punished for having *a notebook.*

These are real people with families and mortgages, car payments and medical bills. But the State doesn't care. Its strategy is simply discipline-and-forget, regardless of the damage this causes the community and the workforce's morale. Say what you will about corporate workplaces; at least there they *try* to pep employees up with meetings, parties, and casual Fridays. In Corrections, there is only fear, with no reliable outlet to vent grievances aside from the union (but more on that later).

Combine this grim reality with woefully lacking communication from management replete with conflicting memorandums, and all that results is disgruntled, demoralized employees never in the know. They come to work every day and neurotically pat themselves down before stepping inside. They wonder if today is the day they get nailed by one of the Department's ruthless policies and terminated for a picayune, nonsensical infraction.

Come to think about it, I should have left that Dunkin' Donuts mug right where I found it and told that old crone, Van der Berg, to stop punching down and start punching up.

4

BITCHLOCK

Disciplinary measures and how officers and inmates
both work to keep things orderly in the communities they inhabit

I t was a beautiful day. Good weather was starting to roll in, and the
bad had finally receded. The sun was bright, the sky was blue, and
while the jail itself was still a muggy swamp, I was somehow blessed
with the job of driving Mobile 1, my facility's outside rover unit.
Smiling, I was pleased with the sudden gift from above my chart
Sergeant, Alfredo, had given me that day. I donned my shades,
readied a smoke, and delighted in the idea of spending the next
eight hours roaming the facility grounds and working on my
farmer's tan.

Anxiously, I waited for the Officer who I was going to relieve. I
had six months on the job, and this gig was typically reserved for
guys with major seniority. This was mostly on account of how easy it
was to perform the shift. Other than rounds, you had minimal
responsibilities, and as long as you didn't crash the truck like an idiot,
you'd be alright. Suddenly, I could see Mobile 1 come around the
bend. It was a big double-wide, triple-long monster of a pickup
truck the facility deployed to guard the perimeter. As it pulled up in
front of me, I couldn't help but view that State-issued beauty with a
sigh of enthusiasm and glee.

"You ever have this before?" asked the Officer inside that I was
to relieve. It was the guy who had the job full-time on the day shift.
He was big, round, bearded, and it looked like years of pounding
Genesee screamers had finally begun to take its toll on the old man.

"No," I replied. "Anything I gotta know?"

"Yeah, fill out the mileage at the end of the night, sign this form,
and take my gun. It's still loaded, but trust me, you're alright." His
breath smelled like a fine mix of Copenhagen long cut and fresh dog
shit.

"Cool!" I said and did exactly as he instructed. Next thing I knew, a State-issued revolver rested at my hip, and my ass sat firmly in the warm, broken-in driver's seat.

"Oh, and kid?" he asked.

"Yeah?"

"Don't crash it."

The officer waddled away to his car, his spine crooked and bent, the result of years of riding trucks on behalf of the Department. He started his engine and drove off. Officers like him were too hell-bent on leaving to re-enter the prison to clock out, but that's okay. He did what most of the older guys on the job did: get someone with an inside post to clock out on his behalf. It was a widely-adopted practice by old-timers who worked outside, or anyone who wanted to leave a few minutes early and had the balls to face the music if caught.

With gusto, I wheeled over to my post. It was a long stretch of service road which lined the perimeter nice and tight, like yoga pants on a single mom. As I drove, I kept my eyes out for trouble, but soon ran into a little problem myself. That service road? Well, it was a little *too* tight.

As someone who grew up driving minivans and little sedans, I wasn't the best when it came to commanding monster trucks like this one. I learned to drive on beater vehicles, and my first car was a crappy 98' Mercury Villager, so for me, pickups were completely foreign. The size and the power of this beast were unlike anything I had experienced, and driving it suddenly became a chore. Handling a truck like this on a narrow little stretch of road with no space to turn around without careening off a five-foot berm was challenging. This wouldn't have been an issue for guys with time; hell, they could drive Bigfoot around the edge of a dime if the State demanded it. But for me, a city slicker whose only driving experiences were in economy-class shit boxes with more miles than an airliner, well, let's say my technique was found wanting in many ways.

Flanking each end of this particular jail were a pair of carports, little covered areas supported by concrete pillars that provided shade and were wired with phone service. Most of the hacks that had this job parked under them to keep the truck safe from the elements and stay close to the phone in case something happened. Well, naive little me, eager to copy the big kids, ended up looking like a child behind the wheel of his grandpa's truck.

With a loud, ear-piercing screech, I scraped up the entire left side of the vehicle in a valiant attempt to swing inside the nearby carport. It was terrible: the concrete had ripped into the clear coat and cut into the frame, leaving a long silver streak across the front end and driver side doors.

My heart sunk. Fresh out of the Academy, and already screwing the pooch big time. Still, if there was anything I did learn in the Academy and from my Drill Instructor, it was that taking personal responsibility often hurts less than getting caught in a cover-up. So I squealed. On myself.

Sergeant Alfredo's face turned redder than his memaw's ragu. He, the five-foot-tall Italian manlet that he was, exploded in a fit of rage to rival Mt. Vesuvius. Through the wave of spit and vulgarities, he ended up asking just how I managed to do something so retarded with a truck so new.

"I dunno, I never drove a pickup before."

"Do you have a driver's license?" he asked.

"Yeah," I replied.

"Then what the hell is the problem!?" he boomed.

He had a point. In the eyes of the Empire State, I was perfectly qualified to drive that metallic beast even if the Department got hosed at the dealership for it.

Sergeant Alfredo then put me through the motions, State-sanctioned procedures after an accident such as mine. I had to go to medical and get cleared by the nurses, fill out reports, memos...all the bureaucratic bullshit one could possibly imagine. Then I awaited whatever punishment was surely coming down from the top. I began to dread the formal reprimand or merciless termination awaiting me. The minutes turned to hours. The hours turned to days. There had to have been *something* up Sergeant Alfredo's sleeve to instill the fear of God into a little new-jack like me.

But no. Nothing. What had happened was technically an accident, and despite all my fears and personal embarrassments bubbling within, there was nothing wrong with what I did. Legally, the punishment would have been uncalled for. Official punishment, that is.

Later that night, as we all lined up to clock out, my esteemed colleagues bombarded me with laughs, crude jokes, and ball-busting to a degree previously thought impossible. I even cleared the whole mess with a new nickname: Crash Bandicoot, a name I wore with shame for the better part of a month. In the end, the playful banter was my only real punishment. That, and Sergeant

Alfredo never put me back in Mobile 1 again. But that's okay. I had my fill of driving. I considered it a blessing, not a curse.

* * *

Discipline comes in many forms in corrections. Some of it is harsh, some of it limp-wristed, but the one universal truth is that discipline always comes from the top down. "Shit always rolls downhill," as they say, and they weren't kidding. Corrections Officers, for instance, can get reprimanded by a superior for seemingly any reason. It's never a rare occurrence, and no matter how professional an officer might conduct himself, eventually he'll get in hot water over something trivial. He may not even know he did anything wrong until it's too late. When a good guy gets hemmed up, there are multiple avenues of attack superiors use against him. There's official discipline, which is scary and career-threatening, and unofficial, which is equally frightening but less damaging in the long term. Either way, trouble is to be avoided at all costs.

Whether it's accidentally bringing in contraband, screwing up the count, or a use-of-force incident where something goes wrong, the State will run down its litany of disciplinary measures to teach you a lesson. If you get lucky, you might receive a verbal or written reprimand. Relatively minor infractions like that typically don't go beyond your immediate supervisor, Lieutenant, or Captain, depending on the circumstance.

Things get nasty when you mess up so colossally that you receive a NOD, or "notice of discipline." In this scenario, the State finds whatever you did to be so offensive that they go after something you have in order to make you hurt. This could entail revoking accumulated paid leave, denying swapping privileges, or, in severe cases, suspension without pay.

These disciplinary measures are sometimes necessary. Not every officer is a shining example of moral principles. Believe it or not, some COs can be just as dirty and depraved as their incarcerated wards, and the best way for the State to deal with these cretins is to hammer them over the head with NODs. Upon receipt of one of these scary pieces of paper, there is always the option to fight it by appealing with the union and going through official channels. If your grievance can't be settled between the union and the Department, arbitration is a last resort: a makeshift little courtroom where a third party dissects the situation and makes the final call.

Arbitration can prevent a harsher punishment if things go your way, but results are not guaranteed. This process is often saved for when the State is seeking termination and won't budge. But arbitration can be utilized for just about any petty NOD, as long as you can endure the lengthy and arduous process.

But in all honesty, prisons can be busy places, and those in charge often lack the time to take a civilized approach to disciplining unruly workers. A Corrections Department is a paramilitary organization after all, and sometimes paramilitary tactics are used in lieu of more "proper" ones.

If an officer violates policy or makes a superior look bad, sometimes the best way to discipline him is to avoid formalities altogether and dish out punishment in a vigilante fashion. While I was never a supervisor myself, I've often witnessed their creative methods up close. Jobs, for example, are like gold in a correctional facility. Snagging good ones over bad ones can make or break your entire day. For example, I was never issued the post of "Mobile 1" for the rest of my career following that infamous bumper car ride, and when I did receive a perimeter post, it was usually low-risk and without a vehicle. Chart Sergeants, who are in charge of who-gets-what on a daily basis, can run rampant on an officer's schedule if they're feeling spiteful by assigning awful duties. They do it to punish whatever transgression might have occurred and to minimize future accidents. But there's no sense in deploying troops to posts where they underperform, and Sergeants brutally analyze officers' strengths and weaknesses to achieve a safer environment for all. Some supervisors will also derive pleasure from sending officers on fool's errands. Any digression could mean counting the floor tiles in the mess hall for a "construction audit," or searching for every broken light in the entire prison. It's hilarious if you're not the victim, and dreadful if you are!

If you piss off your co-workers though, that's a different story. Time-cards do sometimes go missing, only to be found soaked to a pulp in a urinal somewhere. Replicating that time-card by hand is a painstaking hassle but also an effective reminder for a rotten egg that he needs to cut the shit. Disfavored officers may find themselves on the receiving end of crank-calls all night long. Since many posts are isolated from each other, spending a shift answering phone calls from jokers at your expense is painful. This is especially true since phone calls are often critical to a particular job's function. False commands from coworkers claiming to be supervisors are maddening with hundreds of violent cons seething in the immediate vicinity. If a gag is *too* good, it leads to serious security risks.

Runners-up in the unofficial disciplinary awards category include hidden lunch bags, your telephone getting covered in thick blobs of grease pencil (used to write on plastic surfaces, like a primitive dry erase marker), and not receiving a call when a supervisor is heading your way (we call them "trip calls"). There are hundreds of other methods Correctional staff have concocted to fuck over other officers throughout the decades. They all amount to a vast, sadistic database that COs and Supervisors deploy even to this day.

But we've merely scratched the surface! What is a Correctional facility without its full-time inhabitants? When it comes to inmates, disciplinary measures take a much different form, directed by the State to keep their wards in line. And, as expected, can be *much* more intense.

With a problem inmate, the standard method of discipline in NYSDOCCS is to write them a "ticket" or more specifically, a "misbehavior report." A CO can whip these up for dozens of reasons, can drop as many official charges as desired at the end of it. Violations like contraband, assault, conspiracy, interfering with facility operations...these are all codified in a little book and issued by the administration to inmates and COs alike. Thus everyone is *in theory* on the same page about what can or cannot be done behind bars.

Once submitted, Lieutenants and above normally approve them and drop any charges that may seem excessive, resulting in a concise disciplinary action against the inmate and forcing him to attend what is called a "tier hearing." Depending on the infraction, the inmate could get hit with a tier 1, 2, or 3 ticket, each with its own punishments and processes. The hearing involves the inmate meeting with a Correctional staff member, up to and including the facility's Superintendent, and allowing him to plead his case.

The more sophisticated inmates who know their stuff might be able to get off on some charges, especially if they bring evidence to the table. However, most get "convicted" right away and are at the mercy of the kangaroo court it is. Tier hearings have no judge or jury; it's simply an executioner hanging a punishment over the inmate's head that's often pre-determined. Severity of punishment differs depending on what sensitive information that inmate can offer. The more he rats, the more lenient the treatment.

Punishments vary greatly. Lighter sentences might mean reduced phone privileges. An offender might get banned from attending facility events or lose visitation rights. But the bigger the crime, the worse the time, and some inmates might even find themselves "keep-locked." This method is deployed when a convict does something so offensive that he is sentenced to remain inside his cell all day, every day, for an extended period, only coming out for showers and a brief recreation period for an hour before lunch. It's like solitary confinement, but instead of getting dragged upstairs to a secure unit, he stays in general population with the gate locked tight. While keep-locking problematic prisoners is a great way to control their movement, in effect it is negligible punishment. Keep-locked inmates get around confinement by relying on other inmates to deliver items to their gates, passed when guards least expect it. Nor does keep-locking prevent inmate communication. Often that inmate will stand at his bars and scream down the gallery to his comrades, and they'll scream right back.

But for those problems that deserve the most severe disciplinary action, an extended stay in the SHU (special housing unit) is just what the doctor orders. Contrary to popular Hollywood-induced belief, NYSDOCCS has no solitary confinement. There is no such thing as "the hole" or anything resembling a dark room where inmates are thrown away for months to break them mentally. There is, however, SHU: a prison within a prison, reserved for the worst offenders. Generally an inmate will be sentenced to time in SHU if he exhibits violent or drug-related behaviors. The same goes for convicts caught committing something perverted in nature: sexual assault or indecent exposure to female staff, for example.

Once in SHU, an inmate is isolated from the rest of the prison population and must spend a predetermined time in a new cell, one much less comfortably-appointed than his usual cage, while also separated from his property. The offender will be issued a set of clothes, basic toiletries, and some bedding. That's pretty much it. If the inmate plays by the rules, his freedoms are gradually returned to him, and he can even start to recover some of his property, like legal work, books, and magazines. Once his time is up, he returns to the general population, but is often assigned to a different unit, so returning to good friends on the old block is not always guaranteed.

As society "progresses," using a stay in the SHU as a disciplinary tactic is slowly being phased out across the country. It's under siege by inmate advocacy groups and other NGOs for being too harsh, and that the lack of social interaction in SHUs should be considered "cruel and unusual punishment." Bills like the Humane Alternative to Long-Term (HALT) Solitary Confinement Act are crawling through state legislatures[2], requiring caps on the length of SHU sentences and prohibiting certain classifications of inmates from being sent to SHU altogether. The pressure grew so intense that in 2019, the New York's Governor Andrew Cuomo bowed to these demands and signed a legislative plan to "overhaul" solitary confinement policy. This included many of HALT's measures, thus increasing leniency and appeasing the mounting progressive sentiments within the State.

It is a campaign rooted in delusion.

Those who work in the system know: Special Housing Units are the only real deterrent to violent or abhorrent acts committed behind bars. It's also one of the only methods available to safely separate the violent from the non-violent. Even convicts would agree. No one wants a maniac or "bug-out" living next door, especially if that convict belongs to a different gang, set, or prison affiliation and has a history of violent episodes. To allow remorseless repeat offenders to roam freely in general population after only fifteen-day stints in isolation corrects none of the behaviors exhibited in the first place.

Progressive prison leniency doesn't just let the worst prisoners off easy. Notorious offenders co-existing among the more "normal" cons can often make housing units glow red "hot." The extra security attention that high-profile inmates attract makes other convicts more irritable and prone to outbursts. Cons don't like it when Officers are frosty, and they would prefer a much more relaxed environment.

It's also a flagrant detriment to workplace safety. If convicts, officers, and other correctional employees are forced to share space with habitual violent offenders, innocent people become vulnerable to the erratic explosions and furious wrath of such caged animals. In non-clown world, SHU and the security it provides remains a vital piece of the correctional puzzle. Its function within prison should not only be upheld, but expanded. As policy currently stands, SHU stints are issued to isolate the worst of the worst for increasingly

---

[2] "NY State Senate Bill S1623." *NY State Senate*, 9 Jan. 2020, www.nysenate.gov/legislation/bills/2019/s1623.

smaller amounts of time. While it may spare the innocent from violence, it still does little to *solve* the problem. If an inmate spends six weeks or more inside one of these specialized cells, his behaviors when upon release are rarely if ever changed. He is still angry, bitter, and willing to lash out against the world as soon as he is let back into general population.

Instead, we must respond to the depravity of such individuals accordingly. Instead of whittling away SHU time, it should be increased to cover time spans of years or even decades! We need to understand that deep down, these men are fundamentally flawed. They are deficient—not only mentally, but emotionally, and spiritually—and we should start to segregate such individuals into their own private facilities, far away from the men who abide by the rules. Those who treat SHU like a seasonal home should be issued a more permanent residency, even if it means the establishment of more SHU-centric facilities across the board.

But SHU is a specialized form of discipline, and isn't always available to deal with an unruly convict. This is especially true for inmates who incur minor infractions or cause general annoyances. If a convict is playing games on the unit but is difficult to nail on any overt offense, an officer can always hit him where it hurts the most—his property. Depending on the facility, some inmates have a lot of property. They are typically sentenced to long bids and have stayed in the same facility for several years. These men can have an entire cell full of cookies, cakes, smokes, clothes, and all other types of property stashed away in bins and lockers. While there are limits set on the amount of property an inmate can possess, officers usually let these caps slide so long as the inmate stays quiet and doesn't cause too many problems on the block. But that's the catch. If he doesn't, an officer can always decide to suddenly enforce the property limits and expropriate the inventory.

NYSDOCCS policy dictates that an inmate can have up to four "pack up" bags worth of property in his cell. Any surplus that can't fit in those bags is subject to confiscation; it can then be sent back home, donated, or destroyed. Whenever I employed this particular strategy it was effective. It would rob an inmate of his smile and enthusiasm much quicker than a disciplinary ticket, especially if he were a shot-caller or old-timer with lots to lose. Naturally, this method doesn't work on inmates without a lot of property in their cell to begin with, so in those situations, one improvises.

And boy, can one improvise! So far, we've discussed all the "legal"

State-sanctioned methods of discipline, but there's a lot of aces that COs keep up their sleeves if a situation calls for it. When you spend eight hours a day in a concrete box with hardened criminals, you end up reaching into that sleeve more often than you'd like.

One common technique within NYSDOCCS was to burn an inmate on the "go-around." Every day at various intervals, a Corrections Officer walks around a housing unit and takes note of what each inmate wants to do during the day. As he passes each cell, he speaks to the inmates and marks down on the go-around (a clipboard containing the resident roster) and notes whether the inmate wants to come out for breakfast, lunch, dinner, or participate in any classes, programs, or just jump out for television or yard time. If an inmate is a real piece of shit, then there is nothing stopping that officer from simply walking right past that cell and not recording anything on the go-around. This ensures the convict is locked inside his cell for the remainder of the shift, and when the rest of the gates open for scheduled activities, all that inmate can do is grip the bars and watch as life goes on without him.

The only thing that prevents the inmate from getting released for programs, recreation, or anything else is a quick dash of a CO's pencil. If the CO perhaps fails to hear a response, then that inmate is fresh out of luck. The same goes for those who act up and are already out of their cells. A quick, direct order from an officer to "lock-in" after the inmate is already out ends any shenanigans before they escalate. The inmate can't argue against a lock-in; it's against the rules. Either way, it puts the con in a spot and gives officers the upper hand to enforce order and assert authority over dangerous elements. In the Correctional world, these techniques are called a "bitchlock," and they're reserved for particularly nasty or problematic cons.

For even-handed officers whom the inmates respect to some extent, discipline can be applied more efficiently. Some inmates might even tell an offender to stop causing trouble and just shut up, essentially taking an officer's side over a squeaky wheel who would bring undue attention to the comings and goings of the block. But sadistic officers who mess around with the convicts or make their lives unnecessarily hard can find themselves in a bit of a pickle. Other inmates have been known to rally around those unnecessarily being picked upon, taking up that con's defense, and push back against authority. This is rare. But when it does happen, you could see the Correctional Emergency Response Team (CERT) be deployed at the whim of management, and host an impromptu tear gas party.

But that's just the tip of the iceberg. A far more devious act is to use a "stinger." This is usually an old piece of inmate property that officers kept stashed away for special occasions. It could be an altered hot-pot, radio, or television, all of which are against the rules and can cause disciplinary actions if "found" in an inmate's cell. An item is considered altered if its wiring or physical integrity has been tampered with, and thus created a safety hazard. Inmates do this on their own property for selfish reasons; they can make a hot-pot hotter by removing its heat governors. Sometimes they'll create small electrical shorts to whip up a lighter for smoking indoors, which is banned in NYSDOCCS. All an officer has to do is claim he found such a device in an inmate's cell during a search, and write him up for contraband shortly after. It's the prison equivalent of cops planting drugs or weapons during a traffic stop. Regardless, it's greasy.

Inmates also have their own set of disciplinary measures to keep themselves in check and maintain the hierarchical pecking order of housing units. They will often enforce their prison code without an officer ever noticing, and since snitching to security is among the worst betrayals in convict society, victims rarely step forward about it. If a convict is loud, oversteps his boundaries, or insults someone with reasonable clout, he runs afoul of his fellow convicts and makes himself a target.

Threats and extortion usually get the point across, and they'll be communicated in a completely clandestine fashion. Sometimes a troublesome con will get banned from a common area, exiled for crimes against the block. Sometimes he will be made a pariah and barred from eating in the mess hall. The same goes for phone usage. Prison gangs use access to inmate phones as a racket, and will typically place their men on the phones just to take up space, only coming off for those who have paid their way or were approved by one of the shot-callers. Security tries to combat this by establishing phone lists and other protocols to ensure phone access for less connected convicts, but they usually fail. As long as inmates are more afraid of "snitching" than they are desperate to use the phones, prison gangs will run the phones.

I could go on, but you get the gist. A prison is a bad place, and sometimes you do bad things to keep it from degenerating into chaos. That's just life. As a result, discipline is a common occurrence in a correctional facility, and this is true for the inmates as well as the employees. But as punishments for inmates grow lighter and penalties for officers grow harsher, it begs the question of what purpose prison actually serves? Does it exist as punishment for those who committed a crime and betrayed the public trust? Or is it merely an insidious trap, built to gather up as many hard working, law abiding men and women as possible just to place them in front of life changing, career ending situations? The lines are blurring with each passing year, and soon, if nothing is changed, the inmates will have full control of not only the housing units they live in, but also the system that keeps them incarcerated. Their disciplinary methods will outweigh the institutions, and living life as a Corrections Officer will be nothing more than working as a referee in their on-going games.

The line is slowly blurring as NYSDOCCS and correctional departments across the nation fail to dispense discipline in an effective manner. They are failing to keep their facilities in line. They are failing to maintain order and provide safety. They are failing to treat officers fairly. At the heart of it, corrections is failing to correct.

5

Pearls Before Swine

How inmates receive free higher education from
the same people who keep you in chains on the outside

It was already a bad day, not even a half-hour into the shift, and I was packing up all the contents of an inmate's cell. Some dumbass got locked up for threatening to rape a female officer, he was sent up to SHU, and now I was tasked with loading his property into four pack-up bags and getting it into long-term storage down the hall. Usually I could relax until the first count, but here I was slaving away and working for a living. Whatever. At least it was beef patty day.

"Ayyy yo, occifer!" A voice rang out, and a particularly stupid one at that. It came from the cell next door and belonged to a short, fat little inmate with a giant afro that stunk like Muslim oil and cheap reefer.

"What?" I spat, too aggravated to cater to the idiotic ramblings of some street thug.

"So um, yo, Radu had a pussy-book I lent him, can I 'ave it back? Das mah pussy-book cee-oh!"

It took me a split second to process what the inmate had just told me, but eventually I understood exactly what he wanted. In his primal language, this guy, a known crackhead with a nickname around the block of "Professor" (you know, on account of his high IQ), was asking me to return a nudie mag from his now-banished neighbor.

I had seen the porno in question just moments ago. It was a crusty, nasty old rag which consisted of six or seven different porno magazines Frankenstein'd together and adorned with a cardboard cover made from the remnants of an old box of Honey Comb cereal. In it was some of the filthiest, low-rent smut one could ever lay his eyes on. Transsexuals. Grannies. Midgets. The works. The pages were old, warped, and I'm sure you could only imagine the smell.

I shuddered at the thought.

"Nah, haven't seen it." I had just delivered Professor one of the biggest lies of my entire career, but trust me when I say that I was only doing this man a favor. No soul should ever hold such a vile specimen, and now that it was at the bottom of a garbage bag reserved for items Radu couldn't keep with him, no one ever would.

Professor was one of those inmates who never had anything. Out on the streets the guy was apparently a major addict, always bumming cash, smokes, and anything he could get his hands on just to get his next fix. None of that changed once he reached prison, and now that he was behind bars, he would do any little odd job around the block for a taste of his old habits. I once saw him walk on two hands and sing songs for a group of Bloods who just wanted entertainment. It earned him a pack of smokes and maybe a phone call that night, but was it worth the humiliation? If you asked Professor, he'd say it was worth it! He did stupid stuff like that all the time. He was locked up for more offenses than you could dream of, and you couldn't count the number of bids he served with both hands. A repeat offender like Professor would never be the next Republican lawmaker, warrior-poet, or astrophysicist. One look into his dead crackhead stare affirmed that.

Ol' Professor wasn't around long. Fast forward a few months, and I found myself working overtime on day-shift, helping some of the old-timers run a "special event" in the Gymnasium. These jobs always sucked because it was usually hot, sticky, and deafening. The inmates would break out their old, shitty audio equipment from the 1980s and hold speeches and play instruments that blew your ears out in the process. The acoustics of the gym was a nightmare. The auditory experience was akin to getting into a gunfight in a Vietcong spider-hole. Nobody won.

It turned out the special event that day was actually a graduation ceremony. Inmates of all shapes, sizes, ages, and ethnicities had gathered in their gowns to receive diplomas from some educational do-gooders from the outside. As I painstakingly counted the inmates coming in and tried not to lose count, I noticed something quite peculiar in the crowd.

Holy shit.

It was Professor!

With a big old crackhead smile on his face, he shook hands and boogied his little way over to a seat, proud that he, somehow, had beaten the educational system. Our man got himself a degree.

* * *

In prison, there are many ways a guy who is down on his luck can bounce back on his feet. Education, and the pursuit of a credential signed off on by some egghead somewhere else, is one of the most sought after ways to do it. If a brother can get a diploma, he can impress his mama, his baby mama, and hell, maybe he can even use it to run his own business when he gets out. But most importantly, he can use his newly acquired education to impress the parole board and get back into the world quicker than society would probably prefer.

But it's not all college-level programs that are available to cons (although there are plenty of those to go around). Correctional Departments across America offer training that teaches inmates what they need to know to succeed in life after incarceration. Essentials such as: how to read, write, and count. These pre-college courses are all funded by the taxpayer, much like the public school apparatus. Inmates can score credentials in all levels of education, from high school to university degrees, or even learn a trade. Depending on the facility, inmates can learn everything from plumbing and electrical work to carpentry and maintenance. Prison, in a way, offers them what the public education system may have failed to on the outside. With no distractions or any way to cut class and drop out, inmates are forced to earn their high school equivalency diploma throughout their sentence, no matter the age. And they do.

But why does the state spend so much time and energy to ensure its most violent and untrustworthy citizens get a proper education? It's simple. Studies spanning the left-right spectrum indicate that if a convict receives an education while incarcerated, the chances of re-offending after release decline significantly—the better the prison educational system, the lower the recidivism. In the United Kingdom, it's estimated that every pound spent on prison education ultimately saves the taxpayer two pounds. Now that's simple math that anyone can agree with!

But is the personal success of ex-convicts the *only* benefit that comes out of such a liberal system? On the contrary, all across New York State countless nonprofit organizations have been established to help inmates surpass state minimums and earn college-level degrees and accolades. These NGOs are entirely funded by private entities, so fortunately, the taxpayer is spared the burden of fueling this initiative.

Consider Hudson Link, for example. This organization operates out of five Correctional Facilities across New York State, and boasts that they have helped over 700 inmates earn college diplomas and counting. In 2019 alone, their budget (funded entirely by private donors and entities) came to a whopping $6.5 million.[3] The majority of this was spent on bringing college-level course materials into the hands of convicted killers, rapists, and drug dealers across the system. And don't think that only unaccredited, fly-by-night schools would ever get their hands this dirty, because you'd be dead wrong. Hudson Link's "college partners" include esteemed institutions, like Columbia University, Vassar College, and even Mercy, St. Thomas Aquinas Colleges, and other participating SUNY schools.

Hudson Link proudly extols the virtues of its business, claiming that in New York State, incarcerated people have a 43% rate of recidivism (meaning that percentage will return to prison within three years of being released). However, Hudson Link claims that their graduates released from prison feature recidivism of only 2%.[4] But that's not all! On top of higher learning, Hudson Link also supports ex-convicts with "...*readiness skills including resume writing, job search assistance, interview attire, laptops, professional mentoring and internship opportunities.*"

What humanitarians! While you rise and grind every day for a low-paying service job, busting your hump to afford the cheapest refurbished laptop at a Walmart Supercenter on Black Friday, ex-convicts are hand-held through life post-release. Hudson Link even produced a video of a freshly free knuckle-dragger happily getting fitted for a suit by their own CEO Sean Pica (an ex-convict himself who copped to the contract-killing of an innocent man on Long Island for a measly $400).[5]

To be fair, Hudson Link is only one of many organizations established to provide similar services. Take a quick browse over to the website of Human Rights Watch, and you'll discover an entire database of such groups, each with a heartfelt, saccharine name like

---

[3]"Financials & Policies." *Hudson Link - Higher Education in Prison*, www.hudsonlink. org/what-we-do/financials-policies/.
[4]"Philosophy." *Hudson Link - Higher Education in Prison*, www.hudsonlink.org/what-we-do/philosophy/.
[5]Kleiman, Dena. "Murder on Long Island." *The New York Times*, The New York Times, 14 Sept. 1986, www.nytimes.com/1986/09/14/magazine/murder-on-long-island.html.

Children of Promise, The Fortune Society, or the Osbourne Association. Even prestigious New York University has its own Prison Education Program, which, much like Hudson Link, grants free education to the incarcerated along with a slew of other post-release resources.

Operating out of Wallkill Correctional Facility, a quaint little medium-security jail that was built to test the idea of "rehabilitation" in the 1930s, the NYU PEP offers Associates of Arts degrees to every enrolled "student." Upon release, these grads can even continue their education by enrolling in free courses on campus. The only difference, aside from the cost, is they now get to study and consort with all of NYU's other law-abiding students instead of being sequestered in a cell. But the icing on this giant shitcake is that the NYU PEP offers freshly released inmates the *option to meet with staff and faculty at the PEP Office to receive student services and guidance from a Reentry Administrator in the areas of Housing, Employment, Education, and Health as well as to apply to transfer to the Washington Square Campus, or beyond, and eligibility for full-tuition scholarships.*[6]

What does that mean exactly? It means these ex-convicts will not only benefit from free education, but also free housing. Your innocent son or daughter, who worked tirelessly for admittance into an elite university, and which you now have to pay a fortune to keep them educated? Well, I hope he or she likes their dorm-mate Kareem, fresh off the block for selling heroin and copping a domestic battery charge!

While these programs may seem benevolent at first glance (and the data might paint a pretty picture for all involved), scratch the thin veneer of humanism and anyone with common sense can see right through to the sham that all of this is. College diplomas for inmates might be beneficial for the recipients, but it's a quick betrayal and a stab in the back for society at large.

These prison education programs would not be nearly as widespread or effective if not for the private donations and grants that keep their coffers full. But who would willingly donate to something like this? Who would offer up wealth during dark economic times to see a murderer walk down the gallery in a cap and gown? It's not middle class Americans filling the collection plates. It's not rednecks encamped in trailers along the highway. And it's

---

[6] "What We Do." *Prison Education Program*, prisoneducation.nyu.edu/what_we_do.

certainly not the people of the nation's ghettos and inner cities. The nation's wealthiest elites fund these programs, and they do it with a smile.

"Prison education" is a feel-good way for the elite to transfer surplus wealth into philanthropic credibility. It makes for perfect self-flattery at cocktail parties among other neoliberal socialites, and it supercharges the never-ending quest for status in the well-to-do circles of hyper-diverse Manhattan, Los Angeles, or Washington. The elevation of poor, oppressed minorities into glowing showpieces of progress is among their highest virtues, and to work such miracles on a mass scale paints the donors as paragons of moral piety. They merely fulfill their own egos while normalizing the entire scheme in the process.

Do you really believe the average billionaire genuinely cares about the prospects of some street trash crackhead like Professor? He would call the cops the second someone like Professor paused for a moment outside his condo on the Upper West Side, or wandered into his leafy neighborhood in Kalorama. Does the Mercedes-driving art collector in Beverly Hills or even the trendy e-journalist campaigning against "systemic bigotry" actually care if a gang-banger gets his BA in Social Justice? Of course not. These prison education NGOs exist to enable the rich to perform a transaction. Insert money, receive status. Even if an inmate does find himself out of prison, after he gets out, there will be four others lined up to take his place, spurred on by the promise of an easy life behind bars, granted to them by rich benefactors outside.

While the numbers may hold up, the recidivism rate means jack-shit if Prison does not maintain itself as a deterrent to crime. Instead, it must do both!

And what about the public interest? If an ex-convict is educated, works peacefully, and becomes a productive member of society, surely that's better than him running amok with nothing but jailhouse scams and crime tips in his head, right? Yes, it certainly is. I'm not arguing against the idea of prison education in principle. While educated individuals are generally less inclined to criminal activity, those who grossly violate the social contract should not be given free rides while poor, working Americans who somehow manage to keep their noses clean continue to suffer.

Millions of people across the United States struggle every single day to earn their daily bread without resorting to criminal violence. The average citizen's financial security is so precarious that he or she is one layoff or unexpected health condition away from losing it all and succumbing to the weight of the world. Yet despite all this, the vast majority toil on while obeying the law. They never murder; they never rape; they never beat someone with a claw-hammer or rob a bank in desperation. Meanwhile, many work for corporations run and owned by the same elite that fund college diplomas for inmates. These are the forgotten Americans who given present trends will never receive a respectable wage for their work. They will never receive equal opportunities from their employers, especially if they're white. They live as virtual corporate slaves, getting crumbs for their efforts while criminals receive hiring preferences and nothing but applause.

How is this fair? How can a working-class American place faith in a system that stabs them in the back—and increasingly, in the chest—so repeatedly and so gratuitously? They can't. But as Upton Sinclair said, "It is difficult to get a man to understand something when his salary depends on his not understanding it."

Good people are willing to put up with a lot of stress and injustice so long as they believe doing so is for the greater good. But our current society is so backward, the masses barely survive while the select few manage to thrive and dominate everything. This has resulted in a Weimerican tinderbox of elites pushing bourgeois issues like "GMO-grown soy-based anal lube," "laptops for Africa," and "prison reform" while the forgotten American toils under their boots. Our evil elite will dump pallets of cash into utterly unimportant causes while working their serfs to the bone to generate philanthropic surpluses.

If you don't believe me, put on any TED talk. The condescension alone should radicalize you.

The bottom line is that free college diplomas for incarcerated individuals might appear benevolent and, in some cases, work well in the *short term*. But it does nothing to alleviate vastly more pressing problems in society in the *long term*. We cannot richly reward those who have broken the social contract so severely while the majority of those who abide by the law are so neglected. This ruthless neoliberal society offers us nothing but debt and degenerate distractions in an increasingly dystopian violent hell-scape while the media machine lectures us about "white privilege" and "systemic racism."

Besides, does free education, healthcare, housing, and drug rehabilitation behind bars do anything to make prison an intolerable consequence of crime? Of course not—it makes "justice" seem more palatable! When organizations like Hudson Link boast about their excellent work to reduce recidivism, never forget that their largesse creates a correctional atmosphere more like rehab and less like punishment with every passing day. Soon enough, going to jail will be just as threatening as going to the grocery store or a social worker's office. The crime generated by a lack of fear in the prison system never gets calculated and placed on a fancy graph for Hudson Link's website. They don't want you thinking about those things; they want that fat donor money and the social atta-boys to keep rolling in.

Fortunately, I have devised a solution to this whole farce. I was taught to never complain about something without proposing a way to fix it, and our correctional morass is no different.

I propose this: a prison system that is neither too strict and nor too lenient. We must instead implement a "Goldilocks" Correctional system. One that is "just right." If prison is genuinely feared on the streets, crime *will* go down as a result. Not even mental defectives like Professor want to risk being sent to a place with a harsh, fearful reputation. However, conditions cannot be too harsh, or they risk inspiring riots within the prison population. This is a vital societal imperative in the interests of convicts themselves as well as their potential future victims on the outside.

Our Correctional system is far too soft. It no longer acts as a deterrent to crime. And despite the name, it also fails to correct bad behavior among its wards. It's merely a big holding pen, a self-contained meat market that temporarily puts most criminals on ice until an inevitable liberation (even more relevant in the age of the Covid-19 early release). Cons learn nothing from the experience (other than more useful criminal methods), and they are kept fat and happy and often waltz out the door with new credentials for their crimes.

We must terminate free college programs in the prisons. We must freeze out private money funneled into programs that undermine the social compact. The citizenry can no longer and should no longer tolerate oligarchs boosting their social status scores at the expense of the workers who ultimately provide their lucre.

Should we end primary and high school education funded by the taxpayer? No, I believe every person should have access to such information—even the cons. Should we halt vocational education that teaches inmates how to be cooks, carpenters, plumbers, and mechanics? Absolutely not; those trades can help a man more than a college diploma ever could. What about religious instruction and the pursuit of God and faith? Again, no. All of these should be maintained, as it would be cruel to abandon such opportunities, and if there's anything in prison that can redeem a man, it is God.

But the college classes? The diplomas in arts and social justice? The big graduation ceremonies in the facilities and the visits by professors and other *bien pensants*? The transactional feel-goodery of saving poor minorities by the grace of the nation's elite?

It has to go.

We have to create the Goldilocks Correctional System, and ending the prison education sham is a good start.

6

THE FAT SHAUN

*How food profoundly affects the morale of human beings
and how prison food profoundly harms it*

It was an average Wednesday sometime in late fall. The weather was growing colder, and all the windows to the courtyard were locked shut to comply with State policy. The air was thick and stifling, and I couldn't help but catch the unique scent of Muslim oil and the recently flushed shits of multiple convicts wafting throughout. I followed inmates on the bottom tier of the gallery as they were released from their cells and sent up to the mess hall for dinner, one by one. As usual, some took their time and walked slowly, but others, usually the most desperate, raced ahead. For them, their three daily meals were all they had.

One inmate in particular, though, seemed to have everything he ever needed. Books, smokes, snacks. He was from a wealthy Long Island family, and went by the name of Tony Fantano. He was a tall, stocky Italian kid into working out and hanging up video game advertisements in his cell for titles he swore that he'd play once he got out. The moment his cell opened, he raced as fast as he could around the gallery and up the stairs to the mess hall. The quicker he showed up for chow, the quicker he could eat.

"Hey, Tony!" yelled out another inmate; he was an older Italian, this one a mafioso who had taken Fantano under his wing. He noticed the way Tony scrambled ahead of everyone else and laughed. "It's just hot dogs, Tony. It's not like it's parole!"

The one iron law in State Prison is that you don't fuck with anyone's food. You just don't, and if you do, you better have the blessing of all the other convicts. You would think in a place like jail where nothing is sacred, and all manner of horrid debauchery and sin occur, that you wouldn't be able to trust the chow. But you would be surprised. Instead, the food itself is already so awful that one doesn't have to piss, barf, cum, or spit into any it. The food comes pre-fucked, and no amount of tampering by spiteful cooks could make it worse than it already is.

But even though most of the meals served in a State correctional facility are akin to slop fed to only the most deranged zoo animals, miracles do occur every once in a while. That is, judged on a correctional grading scale at least. Hot dogs, for instance, were always a big hit, and no matter how "rich" you were or how stocked your cell was with savories like anchovies or zippy cakes, *everyone* made the trip to the mess hall on a good chow day.

This day just happened to be one of them.

Other big house favorites included pizza, orange sherbet, and anything with rice or chicken. The french fries, while disgusting on a civilian level, could be wholly appreciated behind bars. And especially tater tots.

Food is one of those sacred cows that should never be used against a man, convict or otherwise. At the end of the day, a man's gotta eat. It's a basic necessity just like a roof over your head and clothes on your body. Jailhouse cuisine is bad, and everyone thinks it's bad on purpose. But why? If we are to treat offenders in a "fair, firm, and consistent" manner until they're "rehabilitated" and their behavior is "corrected," then doing so by filling them with palatable and nutritious food would make the process a hell of a lot more effective.

Sadly, our correctional institutions' dietary concerns are focused on one thing and one thing only: money. More specifically, the prison slop complex is structured to jam as many essential nutrients into each meal for as little money as possible. The result is the repulsive jailhouse chow dished out daily across the country. It's good enough to keep the inmates alive, and just bad enough to make them surly.

As a CO, it's frowned upon to eat food intended for inmates, but it happens all the time. However rare, when there's good stuff up in the mess hall, the officers take notice. No harm was ever done by an officer sneaking a milk box or a hot dog. But as someone who was a little more adventurous than most of my coworkers, I can attest that a vast majority of inmate food (especially the main courses and side dishes) is an abomination. The mashed potatoes are always flavorless, the soup devoid of any salt, texture, or joy. The mac and cheese sometimes glows an unnatural bright orange as it's plopped onto plastic serving trays, resembling an extract from Chernobyl's long-dead reactor core. One of the worst culinary atrocities I ever experienced was a horrifying dish called "Chicken Tetrazzini," which tasted neither like chicken nor tetrazzini. In reality, it tasted like...incarceration.

But what can you expect from prison chefs who whip up every meal from industrial bags and mass-produces them in steamy vats? Prison Departments across the country generally import their foods from wholesale sources to cut costs. NYSDOCCS has its own industrial site dedicated to producing the slurry that supplies its many facilities, serving the entire inmate population of roughly 52,000 for a mere $2.84 per person per day.[7] This gelatinous, calorie-dense product arrives to prisons in vast quantities and is eventually "cooked" by inmate chefs in a secure location. Meals are essentially heated in boil bags and then cut open to allow portioning. The process is a New York method called "cook-chill," and it's been the standard in NYSDOCCS for decades now.[8] As a result, this impersonal, loveless procedure makes seasoning non-existent and flavor an afterthought.

Naturally, inmates have developed many sneaky ways to get around the lack of taste over the years. One popular method was to smuggle seasoning into the mess-hall. Prison food may be terrible, but if you pour enough hot sauce, adobo, or garlic onto your plate, you can create something that could almost be considered food. Getting a giant shaker of garlic across the facility unnoticed can be difficult, so some inmates sneak packets of ramen noodle seasoning in their shoe or pants pocket. Once seated, they pour the contents into the meal, achieving an epicurean revolt of sorts against their cruel kitchen masters.

One of the more ingenious tricks I witnessed first-hand was in the treatment of dessert. Most meals do come with dessert; treats like cookies, cake, or a cup of sherbet are not uncommon. A sherbet cup alone isn't a bad deal, especially on a hot summer's day, but if you scoop the contents atop of a slice of State cornbread...*voila!* You've whipped up a delicious raspberry or orange ice cream cake, right there on your plate. I've tried it. It works.

There's also something to be said about avoiding regular meals

---

[7]Hamilton, Matthew. "State Feeds Inmates for $2.84 a Day." *Times Union*, Times Union, 21 Sept. 2017, www.timesunion.com/news/article/State-feeds-inmates-for-2-84-a-day-8761618.php.
[8] "Office of Mental Health." *Cook Chill Brochure*, apps.omh.ny.gov/omhweb/cookchill/brochure.htm.

altogether and shooting for alternatives. In New York, inmates can be "accommodated" with special meals, typically served in response to religious or dietary concerns. An inmate with a rare allergy, like celiac disease, can receive a gluten-free substitute so long as it's approved by medical professionals beforehand. Kosher meals are served to those with certain *religious* sensibilities, and rumor has it that kosher meals are better in every way. Whether it's true or not doesn't matter; this pushed a lot of convicts to request kosher meals, whether they were genuine tribesmen or not. Some of them even got away with it. Guys named "Daquan" and "Tyrone" started receiving a fat slab of Matzah for chow every single day, which was hilarious to observe. "Sheeeit, CO," they'd exclaim. "This chow make a nigga wanna scream oy vey!"

Inmates who couldn't stomach the State cuisine options always had the option to stay locked in their cells to make their own food. Many convicts ended up going this route, and I don't blame them. Commissaries are prison shops where inmates can spend cash in their account, usually donated by friends and family on the outside. They're packed with delicacies like Ramen soups, anchovies, tuna, and all sorts of snacks, candy, cakes, and various other foods deemed junk by most of humanity. Think of a prison commissary like a cheaper, more secure Dollar General. The similarities would shock you. As a frequent customer of Dollar General, I sometimes see the same products being sold to civilians and inmates alike. And depending on the town where the Dollar General is located, the clientele doesn't differ that much either.

When your cell becomes a kitchen, all kinds of crazy recipes start to pop up. Pounding a bag of potato chips into dust and using the detritus to sprinkle onto tuna or anchovies was always a popular technique, and some of the more entrepreneurial cons could even whip up no-bake cheesecakes during the holidays to "sell" to their neighbors. There was always PB&J, the old standby that transcends race, class, and convicted felon status. Jars of the ingredients could be found piled up in cells, and if I were locked up, I'd probably do the same. But if they're fortunate, convicts can even score their own hotpot, and depending on the facility, will even have access to a kitchenette with a microwave. It's a luxury civilians take for granted, but a microwave opens up whole new culinary worlds for prisoners.

While inmates have these creative options to satisfy hunger, CO's have their own unique relationship with food inside prisons. But before we go any further, take note: Corrections Officers can be

JACK McKRAKEN

some of the most physically fit and impressive specimens that humanity has to offer. Many alpha-type individuals work behind bars, the kind who obsess over caloric intake, work out daily, and slay all kinds of tail on the weekends. But on the flip-side of that coin, COs can also be some of the most obese, embarrassing examples of human overconsumption on earth. Corpulent bodies, jiggling in the flickering light of galleries as they walk about, unbathed after several double-shifts worth of sweat soaked into the fabrics of their state uniforms, some of which haven't been washed since they were issued. The common CO is either a warrior or a blob, with few exceptions.

Pizzas. Sandwiches. Entire trays of Chinese food. All this and more gets dropped off by delivery guys at the front gates of prisons on a seemingly hourly basis, and this is a signature feature of the average jail. The COs who order gluttonously indulge themselves on every morsel until not a scrap remains. And this is a feature, not a bug. Some nights working a prison are so dull that eating (and overeating) is the only thing to pass the time and make the night go just a little bit faster. Some officers run into the ridiculous habit of ordering out two, three, and even four days out of their workweek. Thinner wallets and thicker waistlines are the natural consequence.

When I still worked the beat, my particular block had a specialty pizza that was only ordered during "big occasions." Maybe someone just got a new bid; perhaps it was someone's birthday, anniversary, or retirement. Whatever the occasion, we called this pizza the "Fat Shaun," a 24-inch extra-extra-large family-sized pie that featured only three toppings: extra cheese, meatball, and garlic. During my career, I partook in the Fat Shaun ritual only five or six times, and each time I regretted it.

The size of this thing was legendary! Whenever I was elected to retrieve the Fat Shaun from the front gate, I had to do so with a certain finesse. It was massive for a mere pizza, and hot as well, with steam spurting out from the sides of the cardboard box like a miniature Russian sauna. The creation was so wide that I couldn't walk through most of the secure gates with it level, so I had to tip it ever-so-slightly on its side to pass through corridors and enter doorways. And lord spare me if it dropped it: the totem cost over thirty dollars, and crucifixion was the sentence if it ended up cheese-side down on the floor outside the unit.

But once Fat Shaun was back in the bubble, we'd divvy out slices to all the working men in the area who chipped in, sometimes

63

having to relieve posts one at a time so the faithful could join the ceremony. In corrections, you don't get meal breaks or lunch time carved out of your shifts, so you have to make time to eat whenever you can. And sometimes you don't even get a chance to sit down to sate that appetite.

But back to the Fat Shaun: eating that thing was always delightful at first, but regretful later. The sheer amount of meat and cheese piled on that crust was so dense and oily, it could put you to sleep within minutes after the final bite. A single slice was an entire meal; only the bravest men dared eat two. Three slices would place you on a small list of legends that few men can boast about, but chances are those men didn't live long to tell the tale.

These little traditions, as mundane as they may seem, were often the only things that got us through long and lonely nights behind bars. In years prior, COs could cook on the blocks using hot pots, griddles, toaster ovens, and all kinds of appliances approved by the Administration. Officers could plan dinners, and if every man brought in one ingredient, they could be pooled together, and a designated cook could whip up dinner for the boys. It was a great exercise in morale, and we always loved filling the block with the wafting scent of grilled cheeses or steak sandwiches fresh off the Foreman grill.

But like all good things, Administration (notably super-intendents and the toady underlings who serve them) put the kibosh on the entire tradition. I worked in the department during the 2015 Clinton prison escape, in which a pair of inmates achieved a temporary Shawshank Redemption up north, and in doing so sent the media, and the world itself, into a frenzy. Although their eventual capture closed that particularly dark chapter in NYSDOCCS history, the aftermath was devastating to the morale of COs statewide.

The politicians who ran the Department in Albany had a grade-A freakout, issuing untested policy faster than one could say "have a nice day."[9] A litany of new rules took prisons by storm not long after, contraband policies in particular. These indicated in painstaking detail which items we could or could not have in secure common areas. Suddenly, our grills and toasters became contraband, even though some of those appliances had more time on the job than I

---

[9] This is in reference to a note left behind by the two escapees which depicted a smiley face with stereotypical Asian features including buckteeth, rice hat, and slanted eyes.

did. NYSDOCCS now viewed them as tools just as dangerous as loaded firearms or loose razor blades. Some guys tried to buck the system and keep them hidden away in nooks and crawlspaces, but ultimately they lost the will to keep the charade going. Threats and rumors of impending block sweeps by third-party investigators and the Department's own OSI rat squads had officers throw the appliances out before anyone got fired over a grilled cheese sandwich.

In Corrections, you cannot have anything nice. Especially if you're an officer, and this was just one of many sweeping policy changes over the years that eroded morale to the point of non-existence in the heart of every hack there was. Good food, and cooking that food alongside co-workers, was a small but important luxury that we took pride in. But in the end, the State felt necessary to rob us even of that. We were treated worse than the inmates ever were, clocking in every day utterly downtrodden, robbed of even the smallest joy. With such ridiculous policies put in place and without supervisors willing to support their troops, the only thing run-of-the-mill officers had to look forward to was retirement.

The same could be said for the inmates. I guarantee that if the quality of food behind bars improved to something both nutritious and delicious, the anger and resentment in the inmate population would drop considerably, and incidents as a whole would drop accordingly. Sure, you can offer a convict free education and healthcare, and you can offer a CO a paycheck to afford a car payment and a pension after that. But if you offered an inmate a decent plate of chicken and gravy, and indulged an officer permission to cook a steak every once and a while, you'd get a lot more out of both your wards and your workers. A lot more than a belly full of gruel anyway. Or, as decadent as it was, a slice of the Fat Shaun.

7

GAMES

Inmate manipulation and how everyone,
including officers, will try to push up on you

"Hey, CO! 7:30 shower! 7:30 shower!" The shouts and cries of several dozen convicts rang out as they rushed through the slowly opening gates of B-1 Housing, their sweat-slick bodies teeming together as they crowded in before making their way back to their respective cells.

There I stood, several feet above them on a concrete stoop, doing my best to direct the flow of traffic and relay to my partner in the bubble which cells needed to be opened and which needed to be snapped shut. Most bubble officers already had things lined up and didn't need much help during this process. Still, it was always nice to be there for them in case there was any confusion, and on a warm spring night like this where everyone wanted to be out and about, confusion was almost guaranteed.

The nights at my particular facility were always more hectic than the days. This was due to a policy called "free-movement," a period when inmates were trusted to roam to whichever program or recreation activity they wanted, as long as they had mentioned it on an officer's "go-around" earlier in the day. If their location matched what was entered on paper, they were cleared for movement. If not, an inmate could get in serious trouble if discovered by security. Luckily, the system was ironclad if officers possessed a heartbeat and a pair of open eyes.

As the yard inmates rushed inside and dispersed into non-descript streams of multiracial flesh, I noticed a convict named Pepe, a short, bald little Hispanic who was always asking me for something. He was always in need of toilet paper or toothpaste and spared no time in hounding me for it whenever he got the chance. The man was the very picture of a nuisance, a mosquito in human form.

"Ehhhhh CO... Ehhhh I neeed... Ehh... Sick call slip."

I rolled my eyes and turned around, reached into the window of the bubble, and withdrew a sick call slip, and passed it off to him. With the number of sick call slips I doled out on an hourly basis, you would think we were running a hospital, not a jail.

"Ehhh... Eh thank you," he replied.

"Whatever," I shot back.

The night was only getting darker, and seeing as how movement had concluded for the hour, I said my goodbyes to the bubble officer and returned to my chair at the center of the housing unit. It was old and reeked of the collective flatulence of decades of correctional abuse. Still, from there, I could get a strategic view of all the tables, chairs, and domino games that usually sprung up organically every night in the common area. Sometimes it was a surreal experience to digest; as I sat, I found myself beset by inmates. They were cold, calculating criminals on the outside, but in here? They all came off as bored, broken television consumers and chess players. Still, I kept a close eye on them, focusing on hands and faces, watching what they watched, and allowing my imagination to run wild with violent scenarios and how to counter them best if they erupted. All in a self-defense sense, of course.

Whenever I sat in the block, I tried to have contingencies in place for every possible attack against me or other innocent life. If someone swung at me, I'd pull my pin (a personal alarm system built into your radio) and go low. A body hold here, a wrist lock there. In my daydreams, I became a veritable Van Damme or Tommy Oliver, and all around me were the bloodthirsty martial artists from *Bloodsport* or the Putties from Angel Grove.

"Hey, CO!"

A deep, raspy voice cried out from nearby, causing me to jump out of my imagination and back into my plush office chair. I snapped back to attention and found myself once again amidst the human sludge; the television flickered in the far corner while running shower stalls to the left and right filled the air with a misty plume of condensation. The inmate who called out was an older guy named Horatio, he had been on the block forever, and his face always looked old and weathered like the back of your grandpa's barber chair. He was trustworthy for a convict, serving as a daytime porter and total workaholic. If there were anything I knew about him since working this unit, he rarely spoke out for anything unless he absolutely needed it. Needless to say, his saying anything at all was a rare occurrence.

"Horatio, what's up?" I asked, holding the back of my head with a pair of cupped hands.

"Hey, CO, listen the courtyard's real dirty, man. It's all full of ash and cigarette butts; the guys keep complainin' about how much it stinks. Think you can lemme in the slop sink so I can mop it up?"

"Sure. That'd be fine," I replied. Hell, anytime an inmate wanted to clean the unit voluntarily, I allowed it. Sometimes it was like pulling teeth trying to find someone to clean spilled milk, so this was as much of a win for me as it was Horatio. I got up from my chair and walked over to the slop sink closet, unlocked the door, and Horatio shot inside and began filling up a mop bucket with hot water and "soap balls."

"Ehh, CO. Ehhh...I help too."

It was Pepe. He was listening to our conversation nearby and wanted to help out. Fine. Cool. The more, the merrier. The next thing you knew, the inmates rushed out into the courtyard, an open-air recreation pit built into the center of the housing unit, and began to mop and scrub the center of it furiously.

"Wow," I thought. "These guys must really hate that mess!"

I sat back down and continued watching, not thinking anything of it until the next time I made rounds. As I walked the block and inspected each cell for shenanigans, I noticed one guy, a tall, thin black by the name of Kole, sitting on the floor near his stainless-steel toilet. His light was off, and there was almost no property to be seen. He didn't even have a mattress yet.

"Kole?" I asked. "You okay?"

"Yeah, CO," he said, "Just sick, man. My tummy be bubblin.'"

"Where's all your stuff?" I asked.

At the time, I knew him to be a brand-new inmate at this facility, and he had just gone through processing a couple of hours prior during the day shift. He should have received his mattress by now; it was one of the first things you got along with your property bags when you move into a unit. But for some reason, this inmate hadn't.

"Man, they never gave it to me," he shouted. The cell was dark, and I couldn't see him very well from the gallery's lack of lighting. "Lemme show you my paper."

He stood up from the floor and turned his back to me, walking to the rear of his cell to retrieve what I could have only imagined was his processing receipt. But suddenly, Kole slipped, or seemed to have slipped, and landed face-first into the metal railings of his bed stand.

A two-inch lip of metal which juts upwards from the floor where an inmate mattress normally rests offered little padding as his jaw and cheekbone connected with it at freefall velocity.

There was a groan. Then a cry.

I stood there, shocked. Of all the possible scenarios I had concocted in my head, this was the only one I hadn't planned for.

"Kole!" I shouted. "Kole, you alright?"

"Nah, CO," he shot back. "God day-um...my face!"

"Shit!"

I told him to hold on, and I ran back to the bubble, exasperation overtaking me.

"Guys!" I shouted into the bubble window as I clambered back up the steps. "Guys, it's Kole. The dude just tripped in his cell; I think he has to go to medical. It's bad."

"What? Hold on. I'm coming."

It was Tex. Tex was an interesting dude. He was six feet tall, slim, fit, sported an 80's action star mustache, and took zero shit from anyone, convict or officer alike. If any superior officer was to respond to an incident on my unit, Tex would have been my first choice.

We walked quickly back to Kole's cell, shouts of "CO walkin'!" ringing out from every area of the unit. Inmates often did this to warn anyone who might be locked in to stop any illicit activities before a CO could catch them. That could include jerking off, doing drugs, or any other weird shit they might be doing. At that moment, though, it didn't matter. Tex and I were on a mission.

"Kole? What's goin' on, man?" asked Tex, taking his baton and tapping at the clammy bars of Kole's gate.

"Tex... Man..." replied Kole. He was still on the ground, writhing in pain, breathing heavy, and holding his face in his hands. Tex took one look at Kole's bloody hands, face, and white t-shirt and curled his face in a blend of disgust and sympathy.

"Damn, that's not good."

"I know," I replied.

"409, 409, come in?" said Tex, unlatching the state-issued radio off his belt and bringing it to his mustached lips.

"409," squawked the radio. It was the bubble officer.

"409, crack 113."

"Copy."

Suddenly, the gate to Kole's cell whirred to life and opened slowly, sliding to the right. Kole managed to get to his feet and walked with Tex down the gallery and out the main gate. The infirmary was not far from B block, and Tex escorted him down the corridor for treatment. To my surprise, that was the last I ever saw of Kole. He lived, of course, but he was gone. He transferred out the next day as quickly as he had arrived.

"What the fuck?" I thought to myself.

Later that night, as I wrote my report on a wrinkled note pad scrounged from underneath the unit's microwave, the area Sergeant approached and began to give a rundown of the situation. He was a tall ex-marine sporting the world's worst comb-over that had a habit of standing up on end whenever he was distressed.

"Good job, kid," he said, crossing his hairy Italian arms and kicking his feet up onto the desk inside the bubble, nearly destroying the phone that was haphazardly placed atop the surface. "As soon as Kole made it to medical, he started singing."

"Singing?" I asked. "What do you mean? It was an accident; I saw him fall on his face. I still remember the sound it made when he slapped the bed-frame, Sarge."

"Well, it turns out Kole got into a fight before he locked in. Looks like Dappa, Haji, and Radu beat the hell out of him as the yard was coming back to the unit. From what we know, Kole snitched on a Blood up in Comstock, and they made him pay for it. You didn't see it happen, but that's okay. Everyone is alive, and that's all that matters."

"What?" I asked. "That's impossible! I was right..." Suddenly it hit me, a dozen realizations all rushing in at once. And boy, did my face turn red.

Sergeant Comb-over started to explain the intricacies of the incident in painful detail. But by then my brain had caught up with everything, and his explanations fell upon deaf ears like the droning of an adult in a Peanuts cartoon. For those not following, I'll explain it the same way he did for me, and you'll understand the kind of games inmates play on young, unsuspecting COs.

Let's rewind. Dappa, Haji, Radu, and of course, Kole, were out in the courtyard. There, they proceeded to beat Kole's ass in a swift, decisive fashion, the way only inmates can pull off. The fists began to fly the second the convicts began leaving the yard. They were taking full advantage of the sea of inmates all returning at once, shouting and screaming their cell numbers to me, knowing I would be too preoccupied to deal with the chaos ensuing outside. One of those dozens of convicts must have shouted out Kole's cell number, knowing he had to lock in and hide before I saw him injured. This allowed the bubble officer to open and close him up before anyone was the wiser.

When Kole had locked back inside, the aftermath of the beat-down was a bloody mess in the courtyard. Before I had a chance to see any of it, Pepe came on over, asked for a sick-call slip, engaging me long enough for Dappa, Haji, and Radu to scatter into the common area and hide their bruised and bloody hands in plain sight. After I sat back down, the convicts knew they wouldn't be able to cover this up for long unless they scrubbed the evidence.

Literally.

That prompted Horatio to come over and volunteer to clean up the courtyard. Of course, he fed me some bullshit story about there being cigarette butts and ash all over the place, but in reality, it was blood. Lots of it staining the rocky surface of the ground outside. Like a patsy, I opened the slop sink for him and allowed Pepe and him to swab the area down, erasing any evidence of the wrongdoing.

And what was I doing during all of this?

Sitting and farting around in my office chair, thinking up delusional scenarios, and daydreaming my shift away. When I finally did my rounds and saw Kole for the first time after the fight, he knew he'd have to come up with something quick to hide the fact that he was beaten to a pulp. So instead of coming clean and cementing himself as an even bigger rat, he decided to strategically take an orchestrated fall in his cell, right in front of me.

In a way, when I put down on my report that I had "observed Kole fall on his face and sustain serious injuries," I wasn't lying. In reality, though, the inmate was already hurt pretty bad, and the little stunt he pulled in his cell only exacerbated his injuries. In the end, Dappa, Radu, and Haji all went to SHU, Kole got transferred out to a hospital, and I didn't get in any trouble. But from that day forward, I understood that this career was going to be nothing more than a drawn-out mind game of lies, gaslighting, and all sorts of criminal mischief you would expect from career criminals. The only way to cut through it all was ceaseless vigilance.

Or else.

* * *

There's a song that famously states:

"Smiling faces sometimes
Pretend to be your friend
Smiling faces show no traces
Of the evil that lurks within (can you dig it?)"

The song was released in 1971 by The Undisputed Truth, a Motown R&B one-hit-wonder that fell into obscurity after only a few albums. While they may not have lasted long, that doesn't make their lyrics any less poignant.

In fact, the song is so accurate I nominate it to be the theme song of correctional life. They should play it on the transport bus, at the line-up room, in the parking lot, in the mess hall, and even in parole hearings and inside the union halls. In the Department of Corrections, you cannot trust anyone but yourself. Any and all trust, if there is any to be found at all, always has to be earned with others. Whether you're an inmate or an Officer, someone, somewhere out there is gunning to screw you, and when it happens, you may not have ever known it was coming.

Prison is a combat arena as much as it is a holding pen for the livestock of sub-humanity. While we may have progressed past the gladiator games of the Roman era, the tradition lives on, this time in the minds of convicts and the officers who corral them. Not a day goes by without an inmate trying to "get over" on you, scamming or begging their way out of a rule or infraction, big or small. If they can get an extra hot dog in the mess hall without detection, they'll do it. If they can scam a second shower, a free trip down the gallery to talk to their friend, or convince an officer to look away while they take a urinalysis test, they will do it. Or at least try, and there will never be a time when they don't, no matter how many times you catch them in the act or deny their insipid requests. If they have the power to cover up an assault in broad daylight, then you bet your ass they can smuggle in drugs or convince a CO to bring them contraband from the outside. These are evil men, some of whom have the power to mentally dominate weaker minds around them with whichever methods work best.

As a result, a Corrections Officer needs to be able to spot this behavior wherever it appears and squash it when it does. Officers must steel themselves mentally and not get entangled in the games inmates play. If they do, they become pawns in these petty games and place others in danger in the process.

While not the most advanced grift, inmates will often try to play on an officer's sense of fairness and lack of self-confidence by insisting that "other CO's allow me to do X." A weaker officer might give in and allow an inmate to receive something or do something on the block that might be against the rules simply because he is deluded that his coworkers do things differently. Inmates will break out this tactic when an officer goes to enforce minor infractions, like passing items to other cells or not using headphones to listen to music. This works better on newer officers who may not understand how things in the facility work yet, and thus lack the confidence and block smarts of more experienced officers. Prisoners will also exclaim, "Hey CO, you're the only one who cares about X!" This attempt to isolate officers and play on their fears of being different or making waves is highly effective. Still, the older and more experienced you are, the less this method works.

Inmates will also shamelessly gaslight officers, and do it so often that officers quickly develop immunity to such transparent mind games. If you are ever unsure about something, never ask an inmate for an answer! He will almost *always* feed you misinformation, unless honesty translates into that inmate getting something he needs. If an inmate wants to go to the yard but put down for television instead, he is far more likely to kick and scream that you didn't hear him correctly while you did your go-around than take it like a man and stay inside. Cons perpetually manipulate to get their way. They have twenty-four hours a day, seven days a week to make plans and preparations to scam you. With the risks for doing so virtually non-existent, there is no reason for them not to mess with your mind whenever the opportunity should arise.

While these antics may earn convicts immediate, short-term rewards, more patient inmates will gladly play the long con for a much bigger pay-off in the end. Instead of being combative and overtly nasty, these men will instead reach out with a certain cloying politeness and eagerness to work with authority, instead of against it. They will engage officers with humorous small talk, offer their services at the drop of a hat, and attempt to level the playing field and speak to security as an equal partner. These convicts are the most dangerous; they undermine security and gain privileges from officers who fall under their persuasive sway. For the inmate, this could mean the freedom to roam the gallery, or extra time on the phones. Over time, the inmate becomes a confidant, and the officer is now complicit in breaking the house rules and undermining his own authority—and that of his co-workers. Other inmates will take note of this transactional behavior and lick their chops at the prospect of subversion. This breach in security is doubled if a female officer is the victim of such manipulation. If she fails the inmate's tests, she could easily see herself seduced and roped into a jailhouse tryst with a convicted criminal. It has happened plenty of times before.

Once illicit favors start getting doled out regularly, an officer is entirely compromised. If he or she gives notable exceptions, privileges, or attention to a convict because "he's one of the good ones," then that officer has already given up the ship. This failure of discipline will ultimately lead to apathy and nihilism in the heart of that officer, and he may even begin to argue with other staff members as to the relevance of enforcing certain rules. When others observe an infraction occur on the compromised officer's unit, the compromised officer will push back, irritated that he now has to address an issue he would have ignored if left to his own devices.

Manipulation is dangerous not because it gains inmates benefits, but because of its devastating effect on the discipline and authoritative power of prison staff. If multiple officers fall into the mental trap of apathy and indifference laid out for them by manipulative inmates, then divides start to form. Officers begin to develop reputations for being "con-lovers" or "slugs" who "give the unit away." If the staff of a facility does not act in complete unity against the residents, then that facility will descend into endless petty squabbles and in-fighting. This is a huge security liability and prisons in these situations are often giant powder-kegs.

The environment is, obviously, a stressful one. Working in prisons and occupying space with some of the most rancid refuse of western civilization requires a tremendous amount of mental fortitude. It's easy to fall victim to the games inmates play; the stresses of dealing with scum wears on a working man's psyche incrementally. It damages him mentally, emotionally, and spiritually. Sometimes it's so much that he can't help but succumb to the rabble, and when he lays down with dogs, he picks up fleas himself.

But is perfection possible? Can a Corrections Officer successfully resist all manipulation and avoid the complacency that so often results?

I'm not entirely sure myself, but if there's one thing I do know, it's that smiling faces? Well, sometimes, they don't tell the truth.

8

HATE

*How prison leads to race realism
and shatters pre-existing liberal notions*

As a young kid, I grew up in the melting pot of the United States: the City of New York. More specifically, my family and I lived in the borough of Queens, which is by all measures one of the most multicultural and diverse places on the planet. I attended public school in this multiracial goulash with kids of all races, colors, creeds, and even nationalities. Despite our legions of differences, we all got along as best we could; our only major arguments were usually over which Power Ranger was the best (Green, obviously) or whose Pokémon were stronger.

It was a regular occurrence to see me (a big, pasty white kid) sharing spaces with groups of Puerto Ricans, Dominicans, blacks, and Italians all mixed together, just doing what young kids do. It went with the territory, and neither my family nor I ever had quarrels with our neighbors based purely on race. And even if we did, we didn't have the numbers to do anything about it.

Today's extraordinarily racially-sensitive political culture would lead you to believe such a scenario could not exist without rampant bigotry, microaggressions, or hate crimes. But truth be told, they were absent. Sure, we all had our quirks, and things got a little tense whenever a major news story broke about police brutality or illegal immigration. But in those days we were all just kids, byproducts of the working families that raised us and forced us to make do with what we had. We had to deal with the people around us with as much understanding as we could muster, and the same was expected in return. But there was *always* a simmering tension. This feeling consciously lingered in the back of my mind for years, but I could never quite verbalize why.

Eventually, after years of public schooling, my family decamped the big apple for greener pastures up north, just in time for me to finish high school and find my place in the world. While the quality of education and the curriculum stayed the same, the cultural atmosphere was completely different. Gone was the ethnically diverse wonderland that the city had always championed. My new friends were overwhelmingly white, of European descent. In other words, they were just like me.

That vague feeling of simmering tension disappeared. Gone was the constant dread and the delicate social tip-toeing around certain issues. For the first time in my young life, I felt like I could sit back, take a deep breath, and relax. It was a strange, liberating sensation, one utterly unfamiliar at the time. And the strangest thing was that I couldn't even express the feeling, or why it was happening in the first place.

But why am I even telling you this? Does my backstory matter in a book supposedly about the perils of the modern American prison system? We've come this far together so far, but I wouldn't even blame you for not caring about me or my early life. It's a pretty boring affair to be honest.

But allow me to elaborate, in the interest of "race."

Hate, as scary as that word is made out to be (especially to white people who grew up indoctrinated by the one religion allowed in public education: white guilt), is really a natural and rational emotion. While the elite and our rulers bash us over the heads virtually from birth that "racism," "bigotry," and "hate" are learned attributes and the result of bad parenting or institutionalized evil, this is simply not the case. In fact, the opposite is true.

In reality, diversity and multiculturalism, and the idea that our society's strength is derived from the worship and tolerance of the other, are wholly fabricated false idols. "Anti-racism" and "tolerance" are fake virtues birthed in the public school system and continually preached throughout every one of our institutions to keep us distracted from the very reality of nature itself.

These notions may be difficult to hear, especially if you consider yourself an intelligent, normal, mild-mannered kind of guy. Trust me, I was once there too. And it's difficult to deprogram years of racial propaganda, force-fed by the public education system to ensure the serf caste "plays nice" with each other. But there are many places and experiences that can trigger enlightenment to the falsehood of the diversity cult.

Prison enlightened me.

* * *

In the classic 1999 film *The Matrix*, the bald, bespectacled Morpheus (played by a somber, mysterious Laurence Fishburne) offers the lead character Neo (Keanu Reeves) the choice between two pills. If ingested, the "blue pill" will keep Neo asleep in blissful ignorance, and the "red pill" will wake him up to the truth of the world and allow him to live a life of enlightenment. Reluctantly, Neo chooses the red pill and kick-starts a perilous adventure into the terrifying, tumultuous unknown.

Life in corrections or any prison setting is the equivalent of consuming that sanguine medication from *The Matrix*. It reveals the inviolable differences between the races. It unveils the bleak reality of the prison system as a whole. It puts the futility of the progressive dogmas spoon-fed from childhood on full display. Ultimately, life in corrections uproots and upends decades of forced learning and serves as a stark reminder that you, by design, are a "racist" person.

And honestly? That's good.

That's because racism as a natural phenomenon is the unspeakable truth. It is an instinct hardwired into our genetic code as a survival mechanism. Who put it there? God, perhaps. Maybe Mother Nature. Whatever your religious outlook, it doesn't matter. Babies will always favor those who look like them; children will always choose to play with dolls that share their skin color, and even most adults will self-segregate into in-groups that closely reflect our own ethnicities. Inmates do this around the world, and in doing so, make it easier for officers to characterize and profile them on the job. Regardless, we feel most comfortable and secure when surrounded by our racial brothers and sisters, even if we might still remain blissfully ignorant in a sort of blue-pilled miasma. We feel this way and associate this way subconsciously, and no amount of psychological tampering from television commercials featuring interracial couples or from black superhero movies can brainwash it out of us.

A prison is a place where you can figuratively reach into a big hat marked "stereotypes," pick one, read it, and then witness that very stereotype unfold right before your eyes within seconds. It's a place where fried chicken day sees the biggest mess hall turnout by blacks. It's a place where Hispanic visitors regularly are denied entry because they don't have photo ID. It's a place where Rastafarians get busted for stashing weed in the nooks and crannies of their unwashed dreadlocks, and where Hasidic Jewish men are vastly overrepresented in the ammonia-scented halls of the sex-offender units.

Within a year of working behind bars, your understanding of society and life in America (as you understood it via mass media and public education) will be vastly challenged. After two, the illusions are shattered completely. Three or more? By then, your body has thoroughly digested the red pill. You now operate as God (or nature) intended: aware of the differences between the races and completely understanding the truth of race itself. While the *bien pensants* would consider this a bad thing, whether out of ignorance or self-preservation or full enlistment in the anti-white agenda, race realism places you back in a mindset consistent with thousands of years of human history. Only recently did the inane mantras of pro-diversity proliferate; to reject these mantras wholesale places you back in a category of "normal" along with virtually all of your ancestors.

Prison, for inmates and employees alike, operates as a form of smelling salts. It assists you in achieving a mental state which should come naturally to an individual, but no longer does. This is due to the machine working to block off any such transcendence early on in life in order to minimize disruptions to its objective of a homogenized, borderless, pacified global slave colony.

Our rulers understand this concept best (hell, they introduced it!), which is why they spend billions annually to keep the charade of diversity and multiculturalism fresh in the heads of their drones. A career in corrections will not spare you the progressive browbeating, however. In NYSDOCCS, mandatory annual training classes for all Corrections Officers address "racism in the workplace" and how officers must curtail any "implicit biases" that may be festering within them. Working-class whites are considered "privileged," and any thoughts to the contrary are heresy. Any negative feelings bubbling up are bad thoughts. Any patterns detected in the behavior of your nonwhite wards are purely coincidence! A "coincidence" that might be a little bit "racist" must be rooted out before it causes harm to "vulnerable members of the inmate population." You must always be struggling to create a diverse and tolerant workplace.

Can you imagine? As you walk the block dealing with the grim reality of race on a daily basis, your own employer has the chutzpah to then hit you over the head with a liberal cudgel—daily!—warning that wrong-think is the worst possible thing in a den of humanity's worst.

The multiracial/multicultural diversity cult that has taken root is maddening, and even inhumane. The mental and material hoops that white people must jump through just to stay afloat grow more insurmountable every year. While corrections remains an option for the law-abiding white citizen who may be down on his luck, it is rapidly devolving into an impossible racial gauntlet of sorts. It requires dealing with the worst humanity has to offer, shattering preexisting racial notions along the way. But the ruling elite then demands, through official policy, sustained ignorance of the same dark truths that prison work reveals.

Simply put: if you want that pension, you have to submit. Sit silently while presented with blatant falsehoods. Regurgitate lies if necessary. And yes, 2+2=5 when it comes to diversity and inclusion. Want to be a brave truth-teller, and live not by lies? Good for you. But you'll be fired and eagerly replaced by a newer, cheaper, and likely browner correctional unit.

To be fair, black and other minority COs go through the same kind of bullshit. While the anti-white, pro-diversity filth pushed via sensitivity courses may not affect them in the same way that it does white officers, their struggle is just as perverse, if not more insidious.

Black and Hispanic COs regularly play a sad game of social peacocking with the very inmates they're tasked to watch. Because they share the same racial background as the majority of the inmates (some even hailing from the same neighborhoods), inmates leverage this to their advantage. Black officers are bombarded with accusations of being "Uncle Toms," "French Canadians," or mocked for "acting white." All the invective boils down to one thing: if you're black and you wear a blue shirt instead of a green one, then in the eyes of your felonious co-ethnics, you aren't black. You're white. You're a traitor. You are walking in the white man's shoes, taking his white money and upholding his white laws at the expense of black solidarity.

To combat this, many minority background Corrections Officers adjust their behavior to treat those in their custody with a much harsher hand. They tighten up their units, strictly enforce the rules, and even get into shouting matches or outright fistfights over petty nothingness to maintain status as the "bosses" of their unit. He becomes an Uncle Ruckus figure, doubling down on discipline to compensate for the assaults on his identity. He knows deep down that white officers will never view him as one of their own, while the nonwhite inmates view him as a turncoat just the same.

The end result is an officer who will write a ticket or bitchlock an inmate for so much as wearing pants at an uneven length. He becomes a harsh taskmaster who causes so much unnecessary friction in the prison that convicts organize protests. Other, less tortured COs are then left to clean up the messes made by their headstrong and ultra-tough brothers in arms to regain some semblance of the status-quo in the housing units. Black officers must work twice as hard to manage black inmates. The same applies to Hispanics and Hispanic inmates. But for white officers, the power dynamic is inherently understood, and in some cases, black inmates will breathe more easily when a white CO comes onto a unit because at least with a white, blacks have a general idea of what to expect.

However, instead of nonwhite officers ruling as colossal hard-asses, the polar opposite also occurs. Units run by minority COs can, at times, resemble lawless throwbacks from the wild west, with violations and flagrant misbehavior rampant throughout the unit. Some officers even become "friends" with the inmates and acknowledge their "struggles" by tactically allowing all sorts of bad habits. Sheets hang up to shield cells, garbage goes uncollected, inmates wander into no-go areas, and schedules change on the fly. An incredibly shady female CO I had the dishonor of working with would say goodnight to each inmate every evening as she performed her final round at 10:00 pm. She would spend entire hour-long blocks talking to individual inmates in their cells, oblivious to the rest of the unit and all of its mischief. I didn't believe the rumor until I saw it for myself.

Some nonwhite officers will even belong to the same street gangs from the outside! I shit you not. There are many stories of COs going through the Academy with the sole purpose of becoming a double agent, hooking up their incarcerated homeboys with access to smuggled drugs, weapons, and even sexual favors. All it takes is a sob story at the job interview and some bare-minimum push-ups from an eager young female gang-banger for shot-callers to live life behind bars as good as they had it on the outside.

Infiltration by inmate sympathizers and gang members can turn average prisons into glorified extensions of Blood or Latin King territory. They become disgraceful mockeries of justice that only snap together to look orderly if a member of the brass comes by for unannounced rounds. Convicts have no qualms with temporarily behaving and relinquishing power for a few minutes if it means getting over on security just as soon as the Sergeant, Lieutenant, Captain, or Superintendent exits.

I shouldn't have to say it, but for clarity's sake, I will. Not all nonwhite officers are like this. I worked with many who didn't have any of these racial or moral dilemmas brewing within them. Outliers exist in one form or another in every aspect of our lives, and true absolutes are rare. One of the best COs I ever worked with was a black guy named Castor. He was a model officer. His unit was always quiet and orderly, and he knew how to talk to convicts in a fair but firm manner. Castor was just a good guy all around.

But when I describe these prison pathologies, I'm intentionally excluding the stellar outliers. We're talking about the mean. Sure, Castor was a good dude, but he was an exceptionally rare breed. A good Corrections Officer quickly develops a keen eye for patterns as well as exceptions. The quicker he deciphers the different archetypes and social trends within a facility, the easier his job becomes. This saves time, spares headaches, and even saves your lives.

The first step in achieving this kind of social clarity, in which you embrace racial differences and think in a totally "red-pilled" mindset, is to first make the jump and actually ingest the red pill. Our programming makes this more difficult than you might imagine. It requires total disillusionment with prior neo-liberal thinking, often through brutal first-hand experience, and accepting that perhaps what is true isn't what is taught. Only then can you truly wake up, stop fighting human nature, and begin to leverage racial awareness to your advantage.

Unfortunately, the awakening process itself can be a traumatic, sudden upheaval of everything you once believed, and some people don't know what to do with themselves once their illusions are shattered. In our current corrections system, those who are smart shut the hell up and only use this forbidden knowledge as a tool to increase their own effectiveness while at work. Those who are dumber (like me) often run their mouths about their newfound enlightenment, seeking to educate others not yet aware of this strange power clutching society in its semitic talons. This almost always ends up being a bad move, especially in the workplace. Like the carnival game of whack-a-mole, the system is all too willing to slam down on anyone with "red-pilled" ideas, using a litany of punishments, slanderous accusations, and outright insults to get the job done. They are ruthless with their soft power oppression, and as time goes on, they have become exceptional at keeping mouths shut and keeping food off of the tables of those they deem "problems" within the institutions they now control. We are now deep in the abyss of political correctness, with Orwell's *1984* more relevant today than even during the Cold War.

Despite even this, some COs try to hide the fact that they know these inner secrets; some even try to fight against it. Some even kick and scream and clutch their neo-liberal indoctrination, willing to swear on a stack of bibles that they are anything but—*gasp!*—RACIST. But at some point in any officer's career, he *will* become what the credentialed elite and media label "hateful." I submit that they are technically not wrong in their assessments, but there's nothing wrong with hating evil, or opposing injustice. Healthy humans recognize patterns, and they embrace reality for what it is. Take note, dear reader, especially if you are a straight white man who already has a line of guns at him. In this fallen world we live in, "intolerance" and "bigotry" are the capitol sins. And in the eyes of our rulers, you are the originator.

Just take the word "Hate" itself. "Hate" is so often bandied about in our society, and it's usually reserved for one of two situations. You either use it to dismiss something awful, or you use it to dismiss someone who might be thinking, doing, or saying something you don't like. For instance, you might say it when you've had a particularly nasty, under-cooked piece of chicken.

"Hey, this chicken sucks; I *hate* it." Or: "It's so hot out, I simply *hate* this humidity."

Alternatively, you can whip out the word "hate" if you're a member of the gutter press, trying to sell a sensationalist headline, or advance a false narrative for mischievous gains.

"That cop shouldn't have killed him! His heart is full of *hate!*" Or: "A white man killing a black person should constitute a *hate* crime!"

Prison, however, exists as one of the only places on Earth where one can experience both deployments of the word on a daily, hourly, and even minute-to-minute basis! It's a bubbling cauldron of misery that slowly froths and stews forever. And you, potential future white Corrections Officer, could enter a world of hate thought previously unimaginable!

Simply put, there is so much to hate in any given prison. From the paint on the walls, to the stains on the floor, to the industrialized food, to the lazy if not corrupt administration, to the rabid inmates and their animalistic behaviors, to the brutal temperatures, to the maddeningly inane policies, to the antiquated equipment, to the uncomfortable uniforms, to the spineless policies...and more. Oh so much more! Prison is a buffet of hate. Eventually though, you begin to run out of things to hate, and you turn your sense of bitter resentment towards the people all around you. When it does, embrace it. It just might save your life.

And it will happen.

I guarantee it.

9

INTERPERSONAL COMMUNICATIONS

*Rules for dealing with inmates, problematic coworkers,
and keeping the peace in a correctional facility*

Joy was a rare resource for Corrections Officers working within the dank halls of B-Housing. The high-profile convicts who lived in one half of the blue-painted unit were always in need of special attention, and as such, made an eight-hour shift challenging at best. The other half of the unit housed a majority of the department's worst sex offenders: mostly rapists and pedophiles who were, according to their sentences, scheduled to be released sometime soon. Sharing the same oxygen with these loathsome mutants disgruntled even the most positive men instantaneously. Instead, pleasure, or any delight in this corner of hell for that matter, could only be experienced through the smaller, simpler things in life. For me, and many like me working that unit, we could find that simple pleasure by enjoying fine cigars.

And smoking a fine cigar was precisely my plan that brisk September evening, the sudden change of weather lead to the re-emergence of state-issued winter coats from their yearly hibernation. It was 6 pm. I had five more hours remaining in this shithole, and I was hell-bent on spending the next hour of it puffing away on a Camacho: American Barrel-Aged. It was a Robusto-class piece of Dominican-rolled perfection, wrapped in Connecticut broad-leaf and stuffed in the front pocket of my inmate-stitched uniform shirt. I removed the plastic sleeve, punched the end, toasted the other, and finally took in a big mouthful of peppery smoke. In that one blissful second, life was good.

"Davidson. Lock the fuck in. Now!"

Moments later the voice blared out through the unit's intercom system. It was louder than usual, and when I peered through the courtyard window and into the bubble inside, I saw the man behind the voice. No wonder. It was CO Kurt: a big, loud, braggadocios kind of guy who had a lot of trouble working housing units himself. Instead, he thrived in places where he didn't have to be near inmates, like towers, mobile units, or places like the bubble. A "console cowboy," they called him. This type was always a bad-ass behind glass, but a punk who "gave it all away" the second he was face-to-face with a convict.

As soon as I heard that voice through the speakers, I rolled my eyes. He was prone to lashing out at even the slightest infraction by an inmate, and the longer it took for me to get back inside and address his current issue, the more shit-talking there'd be at my expense for dallying. So I placed my now-lit cigar on the windowsill of the courtyard and ventured back inside.

Inmate Davidson, a middle-aged black who got busted for robbing an armored car somewhere in the Bronx, was standing at the end of the console steps and pleading with CO Kurt through the small slit in the bubble window. He looked sweaty. He was a porter who got dropped occasionally to mop and clean the corridors outside the unit or to buff the floors before a big inspection. Today was one of those rare days when he had irregular duty.

"Yo, Kurt, c'mon man! I just buffed tha whole corridor! I gotta gets a shower, c'mon now!" he shouted, holding a towel and bath soap in his meaty hands. He assumed he would get a free shower for his work, and was all ready to hop into the stall as soon as he got the OK from one of us.

"Davidson, you didn't put down for 6 o'clock shower. If you don't put down for 6 o'clock shower, you don't shower. You pull this kind of crap all the time. Now lock-in, I'm sick of dealing with it!" replied Kurt. His thick round arms were crossed, and you could practically smell the Copenhagen Wintergreen on his breath through the glass.

"Ay yo, McKraken!" Davidson sucked his teeth and shouted, looking at me directly like a wounded puppy with confusion welling within. "Are you kidding me? I just worked for y'all. Am I goin' crazy now?"

I sighed deeply while processing the situation that Kurt unwittingly roped me into. The right thing to do was to allow the convict to shower. This was a standard yet unspoken policy to reward inmates who worked hard on behalf of security, even if the gift was negligible, like a shower outside approved shower times. But if I approved Davidson's shower, I would have stepped on the toes of CO Kurt. He was technically correct but functionally wrong in denying

Davidson the shower. According to the rules, inmates always had to put down on the go-around in advance of any showers. Approving this shower would have revealed a clear division between two security members, and inmates *love* to see inter-officer drama unfold before their eyes. Contradicting Kurt would have set a bad example, and I wasn't about to start bickering with a fellow blue over an inmate's unwashed ass.

So what do I do? The moral thing, giving the inmate something he was entitled to, albeit unofficially? Or the ethical thing, locking the floor-shiner in his cell to enforce the rules and uphold the supposedly unshakeable solidarity between two officers? I had to respond. Time was ticking. Davidson looked at me with a pair of puppy-dog eyes and stared like he had just been admitted to the loony bin.

"Davidson, lock-in, let's go," I said, swearing to have a word with Kurt about all of this later on.

"But McKraken..." he stammered, and for a moment, it sounded like he was about to cry. "What did I do wrong?"

I didn't have an answer for him. I mean, what did he *actually* do wrong here? Nothing. The only thing that happened was that CO Kurt wanted to flex on an inmate he didn't particularly like, and do it from the safety of his glass-walled bubble. Now I had to deal with the aftermath and walk a forty-five-year-old man back to his cell like a little kid who just got punished for nothing.

"McKraken, these new officers are out of control man, you gotta get your peoples under control," he mumbled as he entered his cell. The bars took no time in clacking shut the second he cleared the gate. He then sat down on his bed, sweaty and dejected.

"Hey, shit happens," I replied. "Don't worry; I'll take care of it."

* * *

Communication is one of the most essential skills for a Corrections Officer. It's more important than the baton, the pepper spray, or any of other department-mandated gadgets. I found that even-handed, confident words coming from an officer with masculine body language were worth more than a fully-loaded AR-15 when dealing with most correctional problems. And trust me, some days there were *a lot* of correctional problems.

But if this little episode didn't spell it out for you, poor communication happens behind bars more often than good

communication. It's far more common to witness officers speaking with inmates in ways that cause more problems than they were intended to solve.

But if it's so easy to be bad at communication, then what's the *right* way to communicate with prisoners? A prison is a high-tension, stressful environment where everyone always has to be the baddest motherfucker in the room, no matter what. Right?

Wrong.

You might think the best way to communicate with a problem inmate is to communicate a wooden baton one inch into the side of his cranium...but that's not exactly the right move. That kind of communication might lead to trading in a blue uniform for a green one. Instead, the Academy tries its best to inculcate the basics, and this is done via a few classes they call "IPC" or "Interpersonal Communications." After a few worksheets and videos, the Department (for legal purposes) checks cadets off a list, and from then on, considers them experts at speaking with and giving commands to hardened criminals. At least until the next year's training period, when the same state-mandated videos will be watched all over again to re-up certifications.

Like most things handed down from departmental bureaucrats, anything received from these parasites must be taken with a massive grain of salt. In the State of New York, IPC skills consist of a few basic methods likely birthed in a corporate boardroom and then repurposed for a correctional setting. IPC places a big emphasis on "active listening," which means making sure a convict knows you're actively paying attention to his concerns and not just totally blowing him off. This should be demonstrated by repeating the inmate's problem immediately back to him as a sign that you understand. From there, you can deal with the concern however you see fit.

This play-nice type of idealism might work in a corporate setting, where HR has a stranglehold on anything that breathes, but in prison? Hell no. Try telling a 6'5" Zulu warrior you "understand his concerns" as he's about to put a fist through your chest. I dare you. And I guarantee you won't enjoy the results.

The state would also have officers rely on tactics like distraction to keep inmates calm. One of the training videos they always wheeled out featured a CO talking down an angry inmate by bringing up completely unrelated subjects in an attempt to "connect" with him and "de-escalate" the situation. During training, whenever they played videos instructing us on how to speak with inmates, the entire room would explode in a bout of laughter and mockery. Even the training officers, men tasked to sell this garbage as legitimate tactics, would join in too. Not only does this fraudulent empathy fail in practice, but it is dangerous and deceptive for everyone involved.

There are much better ways to deal with inmates on an everyday basis, and none of them involves corporate pandering or brutish violence. The tactics I'm about to share are tried, true, and tricks of the trade that get passed down to new guys upon arrival to shake loose the useless Academy garbage that can only create unnecessary problems.

Rule #1: Don't be a psycho.

This one is pretty simple. Dealing with inmates is fairly easy, so long as you aren't psychotic or a sadistic maniac. If you're prone to random bouts of screaming, slamming your baton into the walls or bars of an inmate's cell, or messing with an inmate's schedule for no reason at all, then chances are you're only painting a big target on your back as someone who can be messed with right back. Inmates will fight back, argue, and make everything more difficult for fickle or untrustworthy officers. The more inmates that witness this behavior, the quicker word gets around. Suddenly you're become someone the populace is allowed to prey upon. Expect lawsuits, grievances, and convicts to close ranks to harass you until you bid off, quit, or transfer facilities.

Don't give them that ammunition. The old adage that honey gets more flies than vinegar is especially true behind bars, but that doesn't mean you should be a con-loving powder-puff either. All it takes is the willpower to not be an absolute dickhead. Master that, and you'll find that arguments and push-back from convicts are almost nonexistent. If they feel they can trust you, even a little bit, life becomes much easier. Cons may be criminals, their lives are in your hands, and torturing them while impersonating a Hollywood prison guard will only make things worse.

Rule #2: Communicate more by speaking less.

I've always been an observer. I find small talk to be drudgery, and there's nothing wrong with saying nothing at all, especially when whatever it is you're about to say is worthless drivel. Instead of all the gossip and bullshit that Corrections Officers engage in, commit yourself to a life of only saying something if you *actually* mean it. Make every word you speak worth something, and discover that people suddenly listen when you talk. A convict will ignore officers who run their mouths or joke about stuff going on in the jail. But the CO who rarely speaks at all can command the attention of an entire room of hardened criminals with a single word. This command presence is a vital tool, and it's worth more than a hundred yacking hacks.

It's also essential to be mindful of your physical appearance. You often communicate to an inmate (and other officers) purely on body language alone. Be aware of how you stand, what your hands are doing, and never speak unless it's delivered from a confident posture. Inmates can smell a bitch from a mile away, and the best defense against disrespect is to never be in a position where you deserve that disrespect. If you're giving a command, then you should stand tall with your back straight, and unafraid to put some volume into it. If you're going up against an inmate inclined to violence, keep a bladed stance and don't back down. All these principles will provide an edge if shit hits the fan, and if done right, might prevent the shit from hitting the fan in the first place.

Rule #3: Give something, get something.

Prison can feel like a daycare center, with every inmate representing a child, each with his own pressing wants and needs. Sometimes, inmates will approach you to ask for stuff. Sometimes those requests are valid, but more often they aren't. It's up to you on how you respond to that inmate and whether he gets (or doesn't get) what he's asking for.

One of the biggest rules I lived by was that if I ever gave anything up, I'd make sure to get something in return. The bigger the ask, the bigger the payment. Not only did this establish a good rapport with the inmate, but it also let everyone on the unit know what I was all about. It set clear boundaries. It let them know I wasn't a hard-ass, wasn't there to bust balls over every little thing, and that sense of trust I spoke about before? This is how I earned it.

However, you want to make sure the things you give are things they're entitled to anyway. Gifts like an early shower or extra toilet paper or a bar of soap aren't hard to come by. It isn't any sweat off your back to give those things up, for, say, a quick mopping of the upper tier, or going out to the yard at night to sweep up the cigarette butts near the phones. This way, not only do the inmates get what they want, but the prison ends up cleaner as a result.

Some COs (especially the saltier, more experienced guys) sometimes give up big perks in exchange for equally big repayment. Examples include confiscated property, packs of cigarettes, newspapers, or even cups of coffee. But those items are reserved for only the biggest cash cows: rats, confidential informants, snitches...whatever you want to call them. I never played that game myself, but witnessed some guys get excellent information out of a convict, and all it took was a box of leftover Chinese food from dinner, or a cup of hot Folgers with extra cream. But caution is warranted. It's not a dance you want to be caught dancing, especially not by the brass.

Rule #4: Never apologize.

This is a quick and easy one. Never say sorry even when you're wrong. All this does is spread the viral idea that officers in charge are fallible and not pinnacles of law enforcement they're supposed to represent. Alternatives to apologies include responses like, "shit happens" or "oh well." If you say sorry, inmates begin to view you as on the same level with them. This inverts reality and is equivalent to raising petulant children.

But there's nothing wrong with being cordial and saying "please" and "thank you" to inmates. Some officers would disagree, but I don't see anything wrong in acknowledging an inmate's good behavior, and coercing cooperation with good manners is about the easiest and safest way to do it.

Rule #5: Never offer anything you can't deliver on.

This one builds off Rule #3. Any time you offer an inmate something, be prepared to follow through. An inmate might be in a jam and need to know details about an upcoming event, or if commissary is this week, for example. If you promise to find out for him, you damn better well try. Inmates are reliant on security staff for a lot of little things they have zero control over, and if you want to keep the natives calm and the unit orderly, you have to be at least willing to meet them halfway as part of your job.

If a typically quiet inmate all of a sudden makes a stink about chow not being right, and to shut him up you promise to call the mess hall to find out what went wrong; it would behoove you to do so. Making a simple phone call and getting that inmate a plate of the correct chow he was supposed to receive (like a diet or kosher tray, for example) is virtually effortless on your part, and the friendly gesture pays dividends in the long run. This also plants the seed of reciprocity, and the next time you need something from that inmate, he'll be more willing to help you out.

Rule #6: Stay consistent.

Of all the rules thus far, consider this one the most unbreakable. Whether you're a complete maniac who breaks inmate balls on a daily basis or an officer who runs amok on the unit and never follows through on anything requested, you better act like that every single day on the job. If there's one thing that inmates need the most, it's consistency. When a CO acts like their best friend one day and their worst enemy the next? That's something they can't mentally deal with. They view the jail as their home. Their community. And if the atmosphere in that community changes on a daily or even hourly basis, it creates havoc. I've seen it happen.

The best practice is to be as consistent as possible for as long as you work in a particular facility. This builds trust and fosters a valuable working relationship with inmates in the long run. It doesn't even matter *how* you act. If the convicts are accustomed to seeing you as their enemy, they'd much prefer that over guessing whether Dr. Jekyll or Mr. Hyde will appear any given day. Unpredictable behavior stresses not only inmates but officers as well. If I'm working in your area, and my job relies on convicts remaining as quiet as possible, the extra stress and drama caused by unpredictable enforcement will flow into my day, and then now *we* have a problem.

If you plan on working a full 25 years on the job, remaining consistent in your attitude and enforcement is a non-negotiable rule. So much so that acting in a "fair, firm and consistent manner" is explicit NYSDOCCS policy.

* * *

Later that night, after Davidson went to bed without his shower, the final count was completed and all the inmates were locked inside their cells. I then climbed up into the bubble with the rest of the officers who worked the unit. I locked the door behind us as we clambered inside; the teeming mass of uniformed bodies gathered together like lemmings. The little control room was filled with knobs and television screens and smelled like a perverse mix of tobacco smoke, hot pockets, and farts. As everyone found a seat for himself, I made sure to find one next to my console cowboy, CO Kurt.

"Hey McKraken, that fucking Davidson is a piece of shit, huh? He's been staring at me from his bars since we locked him in," said Kurt. The fat lip of dip he had packed was still bulging, and the scent of wintergreen wafted out from his drooping maw with every word.

"Yeah," I replied. "Hey Kurt, how long you working the bubble for? Until Cagney gets back?"

"Yeah," he said. "I'm going back to resource on the first."

"Cool. Do me a favor?" I asked, leaning in.

"Sure, what's that."

"Don't pull that shit again. If a con locks-in on my unit, it's going to be my call. When you pull this cowboy shit, all it does is make me look bad, and it puts me on the spot. I mean, Jesus, you could have at least fucking told me!" I said, trying to stay calm, but the incident had been brewing in my mind for the last four hours with no way to vent.

"Why?" he asked, smiling as a thin trail of dip drooled out from his pursed lips. "You a con-lover?"

"No," I replied. "I'm a peace and quiet-lover, and new-jacks like you come here and fuck things up. Next time you have a problem with one of these convicts, talk to me first. Got it?"

"Fine," he replied.

There is a stark difference between being soft on cons and trying to uphold fairness and consistency in a housing unit. Kurt didn't understand that difference, and his behavior revealed his inexperience with working the block. He'd get there in time. But until then, he scoffed and packed his lip, projecting his inadequacies on others and puffing his chest out like a correctional rooster.

But between us? We never had a problem again.

10

OZYMANDIAS

How prisons look, feel, where they're built,
and the mixed blessings they bestow

One of my favorite artists was a man named Thomas Cole. Born in 1801, he immigrated to the United States from England and built a life as a painter while living in the Catskill region of upstate New York. Cole specialized in landscapes, and leveraged the natural beauty of the area as a muse for his art. The majesty of the forests, the verdant greens, and the mighty mountain ranges. The man could encapsulate the very essence of nature within the brushstrokes of his many pieces, and no artist evokes the same feelings of wonder in me quite like Thomas Cole.

Imagine one of his paintings ("Home in the Woods, 1847" for this example). It's priceless and awe-inspiring, and it hangs on a museum wall in North Carolina, blocked off by velvet rope and guarded by men in suits. Now picture a tourist. He's fat, balding, and equipped with a sun visor and fanny pack. As he waddles haphazardly toward the painting, he suddenly trips over his own two feet, sheathed in a pair of rubbery Crocs. He falls forward, splays his hands before him, and crashes into this painting in the Reynolda House Museum of American Art like a mentally-retarded bull. The guards, surprised but unshaken, help him up and re-adjust the painting, but it's too late. The master work is defaced. A greasy, brown-colored smudge has appeared smack-dab at the crest of the hill in the background. The man apologizes but quickly reverts to his fancies, even managing a "selfie" in front of his blunder with an imbecilic grin. The tourist then leaves, satisfied while he searches for his next photo opportunity. But the damage? It remains for eternity: a permanent blemish upon the surface of the work—an unmistakable stain left by careless humanity.

This is the brutal essence of what prison represents. A

correctional facility is to its surrounding environment as the immutable smudge is to the Cole painting: a dark, man-made imperfection that sullies the original intentions of the creator. If you don't believe me, look at the infamous Alcatraz Federal Penitentiary. It's an ugly, foreboding megalith of misery, smack dab in the center of the idyllic San Francisco Bay. Or take the famous Attica Correctional Facility, whose lily-white walls stand defiant in proximity to the resplendent nature of our northern neighbor, Canada.

The United States is replete with aesthetic atrocities like these, and the State of New York is no exception. This is a tragedy, considering New York contains a continent's worth of natural beauty just within its limited borders. It's not difficult to drive through any of our interstates or state roads and observe the majesty of foothill vistas and splendorous forests temporarily marred by concrete hulks lined with metallic wire. There's something about the physical appearance of prisons and jails that instill a sense of dread in the observer. Whether that effect is by design or an incidental result derived from pondering the purpose of the facilities is beyond me. Either way, the dread is inescapable.

These blotches on nature come in many shapes, colors, and sizes, and they can be as varied and diverse as the inmates who are stored within. New York classifies its facilities into categories such as minimum, medium, and maximum. The higher the security, the darker the souls that dwell inside. During my career, I worked at a medium-security facility and a maximum one. While the differences in policy and procedure between the two were staggeringly different, the misery within was roughly the same. I compared it to ice cream; you can have chocolate or vanilla, but you're still biting into a cone at the end of the day.

Medium security prisons often look like large summer camps but with cabins and campfires replaced by barbed wire fences and the lingering aroma of rollie cigarettes. Inmates are sentenced to specific prions based on the severity of their crimes. As a result, medium security inmates enjoy a greater level of trust than those condemned to maximum alternatives. Medium security inmates typically live in a communal, dormitory-style housing unit with no bars or cells, and have cubicle-style bunk areas complete with access to a television room and a lot more living space.

Medium security prisons offer more freedom as well. This comes in one form via a kitchenette area, where inmates can cook their meals and even use a microwave (a luxury maximum security inmates could only ever dream of having). There's also a greater emphasis on programs like vocational studies, guidance, counseling, and even family development classes. And depending on the facility, some minimum facilities even have programs which center on temporary release, a valuable and highly desired reward which requires a great deal of consistent good behavior from convicts before being granted. There's a lot more carrot than stick in a medium security joint, and thus things tend to be more laid back. It's still miserable, but the chances of being caught up in violence are greatly diminished.

Maxes are a different story, and these massive structures pock-mark the great State of New York like a bad case of shingles. Infamous facilities like Attica or Sing-Sing usually come to mind when one thinks of a New York prison, and those places are still very much alive and kicking today. Maximum security prisons are the ones where you would see stereotypical prison themes. Small, claustrophobic cells, old iron bars, guard towers, and yard time. Shank attacks and tear gas. These prisons hold the most dangerous men in our civilization, and as a result they need to be prepared for violence, 24/7.

The maximum prison I worked was an architectural wonder and a jailer's wet-dream. Built in the 1980s as an impregnable fortress, this particular facility had more strategic deterrents to escape integrated in its design than most. You couldn't enter or exit the facility without passing through multiple slow-moving, remotely controlled gates operated from a secure location elsewhere on the property (usually called the Arsenal). Each area of this facility was divided into multiple quadrants, with each quadrant controlled remotely from a control center at the center of the unit (i.e., the Console or "bubble".) If the inmates were to completely take control of one of the quadrants, they would somehow have to liberate the neighboring quadrant just to inch closer to the main exit. In addition, prospective escapees would only be met with the final obstacle: a long, narrow corridor the length of a football field. This corridor led directly to the front door, and ultimately freedom, but could be re-purposed as a kill-zone for the armed men stationed at the gates at a moment's notice in any emergency.

This design creates a veritable gauntlet for the latent force of inmate rioters seeking escape, and defends the public from the potential marauders within. While each prison may look and feel wildly different (Sing Sing was built in 1828, for example), the core of their designs all reflect the same intent: certain doom for the escape artist. The only chink in the departmental armor lies in the older, historical prisons. These rotting tombs of American history would be better served as museums then prisons at this point, and their weakness was never more on display then during the 2015 Clinton prison escape. This caper, which lasted three weeks and cost the State of New York $25 million, saw two inmates make a complete mockery of the Department of Corrections. Their names were Richard Matt (a knife murderer) and David Sweat (a cop-killer.) After cutting through metal and digging their way out of the deteriorating infrastructure of Clinton Correctional Facility[10] (built in 1844), they were finally captured after one had been killed and the other air-holed by law enforcement near the Canadian border. While Sweat still lives behind bars under close supervision, so too does the idea that these prisons have vulnerabilities despite their impeccable designs.

But what to do about it? America has an obvious problem with crime. If it didn't, there wouldn't be a need for *so many* prisons, including the upkeep of antiquated ones as well as the constant construction of new ones. Cutting crime by providing better living standards and employment opportunities is a better and more obvious alternative. But this has been tried since at least LBJ's Great Society programs of the 1960s, and we are reminded of the failures of such efforts daily. How much money, time, education, and effort must we pour into inner-cities to cure the deviants who conduct the majority of violent crimes? To paraphrase Marlon Brando in *The Wild One*, "how much you got?!" But this maddening prison industrial complex *does* provide a hidden benefit. If a magic wand were to be waved and crime magically reduced, what would happen to the countless upstate communities that rely on prisons as sources of income? New York State corrections currently employs approximately 31,000 individuals, the majority of whom are white, upstate ruralites who live close to the prisons and have little other stable employment prospects. I am a living embodiment of this reality. Minimize the jails, and many of the towns, villages, and families who dwell near them risk imminent disaster and the chance

---

[10]"How Two Prisoners Escaped From A Maximum Security Prison." *The New York Times*, The New York Times, 8 June 2015, www.nytimes.com/interactive/2015/06/08/nyregion/prison-escape.html.

of vanishing altogether, just like the countless working class neighborhoods decimated by the crime of the inmates populating the prisons.

And what of the budget? In New York State, the Department of Corrections and Community Supervision owns and operates its own corrections company aptly named "Corcraft." Their mission statement: "To employ inmates in substantive jobs that help teach a good work ethic and valuable work skills, to help offset the cost of incarceration, to help reduce disruption in the prison environment, and to meet expectations of New York State's citizens." But behind the weasel words and saccharine platitudes, Corcraft brings in millions of dollars annually for the State by selling products made in prisons to customers of all stripes. New York prison products include furniture, textiles, clothing, office supplies, laundry detergent, cleaning materials, and even highway and traffic signage.

According to reporting by the New York City news outlet Gothamist, "Corcraft averages around $48 million in sales annually." This revenue is achieved largely thanks to New York State Finance Law STF § 162,[11] which mandates that all local governments must purchase items from Corcraft if it happens to sell that particular item. This means that the NY DMV must order hand soap from Corcraft. The same goes for municipal city buildings in need of new furniture, county clerk offices needing new office supplies, and towns that need new street signs. We can put things into further perspective by understanding that NYS prisons were allocated $69 million dollars in 2020,[12] and the investment, it seems, makes for a good return on the money spent.

This income, while valuable for the State, doesn't come without serious human cost. Corcraft can only produce these goods by leveraging a resource that would make most capitalists lust with envy. That resource, of course, is prison labor. By paying incredibly low wages averaging a little over a thousand dollars per year per inmate, the State squeezes as much money as they can out of an industry wholly built on the backs of what can be considered slave labor. Depending on the job, inmates are paid as little as 16 cents per hour.

---

[11] "New York Consolidated Laws, State Finance Law - STF § 162." *Findlaw*, codes.findlaw.com/ny/state-finance-law/stf-sect-162.html.
[12] "2020-2021 Executive Budget." *Department of Corrections and Community Supervision*, 12 Feb. 2020, doccs.ny.gov/news/2020-2021-executive-budget.

What we're left with is a tragic comedy and a brutal Catch-22. If crime were to diminish, the prisons would recede with it, no longer proliferating as dark smudges on the Thomas Cole painting we call America. But without them, we would lose not only a boon to the state budget, but entire communities and livelihoods. Tens of thousands of "free" New Yorkers rely on the toxic industry that is the New York State prison system, and it seems unfair to deny their right to live and work in a world that seems to thrive off of the suffering of our fellow man.

It's a difficult choice, but I know what I would do.

If a supreme being granted me the omnipotence to exact a single change on the American prison system, it would not take me long to strike. With the flick of a wrist, I would condemn all prisons in the nation's rural areas, and relocate them to the major cities where the vast majority of criminals originate. This would infuriate the urbanite do-gooders who nevertheless are always quick to shout NIMBY ("not in my backyard!"). But to hell with them. I would make a super-max prison out of the Freedom Tower in Manhattan. I would make a minimum-security work-release unit out of the Plaza Hotel, and I would erect a dungeon in the barred husk of Madison Square Garden. Urban areas are already hectic, cast in the shadows of corruption, and full of scum and grime, and would thus be the natural setting to house their vile offspring. Once unmarred beauty is restored to the vast wilderness to the north and west of Gotham, we could then shift our focus and start to rebuild, and find new purpose for upstate communities who would stand to lose the most from this sudden change. Together, we could seek new, exciting industries to save our towns, with work more noble and respectable than prison exploitation and the darkness of working behind the fence.

And our Thomas Cole painting? It would be smudge-free.

Immaculate and perfect.

11

KEY CONTROL

The most important tool of Corrections Officers
and how little it's respected

It was April when I first arrived at a real-life State Prison. The air was filled with a sweet, springtime aroma, and the sun had started to shine down upon the emerald-green valley where this particular super-max was built just a few decades prior. I was fresh out of the Academy back then. You could tell pretty easily too. My shirts were still starched and crisply ironed, my boots were still gleaming from polish, and my spirits were still high.

I had just undergone two days of what was known as "orientation." During this brief training, I was introduced to the facility's policies and procedures and escorted to secure areas to meet the varied characters in charge of the whole operation. Once the formalities were complete, and after signing a bible worth of admittance papers and shaking more hands than I could count, all of us new guys were escorted "down back." It was here we were finally away from the cozy offices upfront to meet and greet our fellow officers holding the line, and tour the areas where we would be toiling for what could be years.

One of the first stops was A-Block (or Alpha block if you're military-minded). This was a cookie-cutter duplication of all of the other blocks in the jail, but what made it unique was the particular clientele working the beat. On day shift, the six or seven guys working in the unit had, collectively, more seniority than God. They were older, unshaven, and could retire faster than they could be fired. As a result, they had an edge that most of the other officers I had met so far seemed to lack. They were invincible, or so they believed, and displayed their bravado openly in a place like A-Block with complete disregard for anyone who might enter their realm. Even the brass.

This "fuck you" attitude was doubly applied to new guys like me.

"Heeeeey! There he is!" a few of them bellowed as we stepped inside the nearly pristine bubble that sat at the center of A-Block. The men were shouting to CO Kelly, the officer in charge of giving us the tour of the facility, to which he merely raised his hand in a disinterested hello. I did my best to smile and not draw negative attention to myself. "Top of the morning to ya, ya mick fuck."

"I come bringing a few o' me leprechauns!" Kelly replied in an Irish accent of his ancestors, or at least a poor facsimile of one. "Everyone welcome our new OJTs! OJTs, these are the hacks from Alpha block, hacks from Alpha block, these are the OJTs."

"Hello, everyone!" said one of my newly hired compatriots, his hair slicked back and his collar-brass gleaming in the overhead light of the console. "What's going on?"

"Oh, you know," replied CO Kowalski, a gruff, fat, Polack whose belly was barely contained by the leather of his state-issued belt. "Just livin' the dream."

"Yeah, kids. Just havin' another fun-filled morning," replied another. This was CO Schroder, a tall, lanky female with the blonde hair of a beauty queen and the eyes of a medicated psychopath. The sarcasm in her words was so thinly-veiled you could cut it with a mess hall spatula. "Hey you, the big one. Close the door, will you? Make sure it's locked."

My eyes widened when I realized she was speaking to me. I was the one standing closest to the console door: a big steel slab fitted with bulletproof glass window panes and hinges the size of a human hand. Resting in the door's keyhole was a set of bit keys, giant brass monstrosities that were custom-made for prison use and standard for every critical area of the facility. Usually they were left in the keyhole of the bubble door on purpose. If someone left the bubble, someone inside the bubble had to close and lock the door behind them. Since the bubble controlled all of the main gates and the cell doors on the unit, locking and securing that door was of the utmost importance. Because of this, you always had to have at least one man in the bubble at all times. If the bubble was lost, the unit was lost.

I responded to Schroder's request as quickly as possible, pressing the heavy door closed and taking the bit keys in my hand. As I turned the master key to lock the door, it met unexpected resistance. To my surprise, it wasn't locking.

I turned the key and tried again. And again. And then again. Each time I was met with a frustrating blockage of some sort—an unsatisfying "thump" resonating with each attempt.

"Weird," I said. "It's not locking."

"Keep trying, kid," said CO Williams, clearly the oldest man on the unit. He had a silvery-white mane, varicose veins in his arms and hands, and a voice like sandpaper, evidence of years of torture by cheap gas station cigarettes. "That one's a bitch, just like my ex-wife."

So I kept trying, but I was greeted with embarrassing failure with each attempt. I could feel my face getting redder. The first day on the job and I was proving to a whole room of correctional veterans that I couldn't even close and lock a door! It was the most basic functions of a prison guard, for Christ's sake, and I couldn't even do that right!

"Hey kid, don't force it!" barked Kowalski, his laughter growing louder with each passing moment. Chuckles from the others started to sneak in as well, watching with eager eyes the sight of a new-jack struggle with something they had all mastered decades ago. "Just be gentle with it, like a nine-year-old's pussy."

The laughter erupted into a veritable howl; even Schroder was beside herself. But the words hit me over the head like a ball-pein hammer. Never had I heard something so degenerate come out of someone so unassuming. Surprisingly enough, the advice, vile as it was, seemed to work! Instead of forcing the key to spin to the right, I gently turned it in one fluid motion. It made its way in a semi-circle fashion to its natural completion and emitted a satisfying "click." Finally the door was locked, and the area secured.

*   *   *

A big part of working in any correctional capacity involves keys. Almost every area of a facility, from the smallest corridor to the largest housing unit, will have a set of keys that correspond with it. In some cases, one area may even have two or three sets depending on its needs. Since security is at the heart of the profession, an officer must keep track of and be held accountable for the keys on his person at every waking moment. If he loses one or gives them to another officer and forgets, well, then he can find himself in some really big trouble. The same applies if he fails to keep a room locked, an area closed, or breaks them altogether. (This does occur. These key-rings can sometimes be ancient pieces of metal to rival Arthurian steel.)

If an officer practices what the department refers to as "Key

Control," then these workplace mishaps shrink to a minimum, leaving a facility, area, and career safe from harm. Key control sounds like it should be self-explanatory, but the New York State Department of Corrections and Community Supervision still feels the need to devote an entire segment of their Academy classwork to the proper (and improper) use of keys while on the job.

In these short-lived classes, an officer learns all sorts of super-secret state-developed methods to keep those keys safe. For one, always keep your keys secured on your state-issued "key clip" unless you're ready to *actually* use them. Key clips are stainless steel, belt-worn clips that you can use to snap a ring of keys to. While attached, it's nearly impossible to remove a key-ring from an outside source (i.e., an inmate), and you never have to worry about misplacing your keys or having them fall out of a pocket or something. Sure, they might jingle on your belt all day as you walk about the facility, but the feeling of ease one gets from knowing those keys are safe and sound by your hip is a level of comfort that you didn't know you needed. In fact, they are so useful that I even bought my own clip that I continue to use today as a civilian.

Another big tip they issue young recruits is this: when passing keys off to a relieving officer, always hand them to that officer in an orderly fashion. This means refraining from throwing, chucking, or tossing your keys across a room to someone, simply because you were too lazy to walk an extra step closer. In the Academy, we were always bombarded with horror stories. These involved officers performing wild toss-offs which resulted in a set of keys falling down a storm drain, off of the ledge of a tower, or into the hands of a scheming inmate nearby. All of which can result in severe discipline or even termination. In the correctional world, keys are no joke. It's best to take them seriously.

But do COs ever heed this advice?

Hell no!

Once you're working behind bars, all of these useful tips go straight down the toilet. Within the first few hours working inside a prison, I witnessed so many instances of inadequate key control it made my head spin.

COs will throw key-rings across a crowded gymnasium.

COs will lend their keys out so other officers can use a nicer bathroom.

COs will leave their keys and even radios out on a desk as they await relief.

COs will leave keys placed in the keyhole of a critical door unsupervised.

Hell, COs will even fail to report a bent, broken, or missing key just because they might have to work overtime and submit an incident report.

Consider how archaic some of the locking mechanisms in the doors of these correctional facilities are. If my previous story about A-Block wasn't an indicator, doors in a state prison are sometimes so old and poorly maintained that you never knew just how each lock would respond until you tried it for the first time. Some locks were so bad that only seasoned bid officers had the know-how to lock or unlock a specific door. Sometimes there were so many keys on your key-ring that new officers or new-jacks found themselves completely baffled as to what went where.

It was a common occurrence to stand before a locked closet door and use every single key on the ring until finding the correct one. Inmate porters often knew which key to use before an officer did, and had no problem telling those officers which key on the ring was the right one! This saved the officer embarrassment, and the inmate, the time of waiting for an officer who might fumble around for five minutes. Pathetic!

This is simply not a professional way to work in a state prison, but it's the unfortunate reality of the situation. You can get jammed up pretty bad for misplacing keys or exhibiting poor key control on the job, and if you decide to join the Department, shave your beard and gain the obligatory fifteen pounds that go along with your newly minted badge, you wanna keep a close eye on your keys.

Just be gentle with them.

Those locks can be a bitch, just like William's ex-wife.

12

LAWFARE

*How inmates wage war on
a system that doesn't fight back*

I hate convicts. Anyone who takes on the badge and dons the blue may not admit it openly, but in secret they will tell you the same thing. But when you ask officers *why* they hate convicts, the answer will never be the same. Some COs will remark on their smell –skin covered thickly in "Muslim oil" (a noxious perfume obtained only for religious purposes that seems to mysteriously end up in the hands of inmates of all denominations). Some COs will comment on their language, which is filled with street slang, profanity, and not a single triple-syllable word in their entire vocabulary. Some COs will hate them merely for the crimes they committed, and it's common to meet officers who will give baby-rapists and pedophiles a much harder time.

Good for them. There's a special place in hell for those monsters, and I don't necessarily care if their torment starts a little early.

But what do I hate most about convicts? It's a simple answer. It's their entitlement.

Every convict I've ever met, from the run-of-the-mill gang-banger to the common drug-addled wife-beater, all walk around prison with a certain sense of entitlement lacking in the most regal of monarchs. They act invincible. Pure. As if the crimes they committed and the inmate status they received somehow grants them a protection in our society. And in some way they're not wrong. But in reality, they only enjoy those protections to prevent law-abiding people like you and me from getting fed up and smashing their skulls in with fire extinguishers.

But what causes this entitlement? What creates this uppity air of conceit in the hearts of the nation's worst offenders? I'd be lying if I said I didn't think about this at least once a day when I was on the job. Many of the other guys did too, or at least the ones I felt comfortable confiding with. But we always came to the same conclusions.

These motherfuckers are just spoiled.

Despite being sentenced to prison as punishment for their crimes, many of these individuals are treated better *behind* bars than they ever were *outside*. State inmates, as a condition of their time spent locked away, will receive all kinds of benefits that many never had back home. Once in state custody, these men and women are guaranteed three meals a day and medical attention almost any time for seemingly any ailment, minor or major. They receive access to groceries, toiletries, near-limitless visitation rights from family and friends back home. They receive care packages, phone calls, and electronic tablets with access to e-mail and downloadable content which they can purchase from unit-based "kiosks." They receive guaranteed recreational time, schooling, psychiatric treatment, and addiction counseling. They receive televisions inside and out of their cells, radios, group events, and the ability to fuck their wives and breed new criminals. All on the state's dime!

They can't leave, fight, drink, or use drugs, but most normal, level-headed individuals would consider that a decent trade considering the dozens of state-offered amenities offered in return.

As a taxpayer, I know I would. Some days, it even seemed enticing!

But the biggest slap in the face to every citizen of this country is that these inmates, who are supposed to be doing "hard time" for "hard crime," continue scamming polite society and making money on the inside. And lots of it! All that's required to score beaucoup bucks behind bars is a little finesse, a cranky attitude, and some good old fashioned *lawfare*.

What's lawfare, you might ask? It's the practice of using society's laws for nefarious purposes. A form of judicial judo, lawfare harnesses a civilization's standards, values, and codified rules to attack a target, shut it up, lock it up...or profit from it. It's a devious deed that only a criminal could perpetrate without feeling existential guilt, but incarcerated criminals don't lose the criminal mindset. At least, not in today's Correctional Departments.

Before we get into the different kinds of lawfare and how inmates get away with it, let's rewind a bit for the story of a little place called Attica.

September 1971 was a Waterloo for Attica Correctional Facility.

This white-walled dungeon is located east of Buffalo in New York's Wyoming County and was the repository for the State's most heinous scum. At the time, Bill Wither's "Ain't No Sunshine" was topping at number three on Billboard's Hot 100, but more importantly, the prison had just undergone a violent takeover by the inmate population. With guards held hostage and negotiations breaking down, Governor Nelson Rockefeller (a liberal old-money Republican) ordered that the facility be taken back by force. The initial violence was met with even more violence, as the National Guard and State Police beat, gassed, and shot their way through Attica, crushing the uprising four days after it began.[13] When the bullets quit flying and the CS gas cleared from the corridors and yards, the resulting damage was staggering. At least forty-three people, including thirty-three convicts and ten corrections personnel, lay dead. And that was just the human toll. There were millions of dollars in property damage, as well as countless liability claims to the State.[14] The losses on both sides of the conflict led to legal reverberations that are still relevant today.

It was such a shocking, visceral, and viral news story that something had to be done as a result.

In the wake of "Attica," public trust in the State and its law enforcement apparatus collapsed, and the system couldn't allow another dangerous humiliation to occur. So the politicians conceded and gave the people (and inmates) most of what they wanted to return to the status quo. The New York State Department of Corrections adopted a few major policy changes,[15] many of which were rational, like daily showers for inmates (up from only one per week) and expanded religious freedoms. But some led to a sea change in the general liberty of the incarcerated class.

For one, inmates were given a brand-new grievance procedure. This allowed any inmate to object to prison processes that might violate directives or policies. COs and administrators could no longer make up the rules on the fly. As long as an inmate was willing to complete paperwork to push back against the system that kept

[13]Getlen, Larry. "The True Story of the Attica Prison Riot." *New York Post*, New York Post, 20 Aug. 2016, nypost.com/2016/08/20/the-true-story-of-the-attica-prison-riot/.
[14]*CNN*, Cable News Network, edition.cnn.com/2000/US/01/04/attica.settlement/.
[15]Press-Republican, Kim Smith Dedam. "After Attica: Inmate Uprising Leads to Reform." *Press*, 17 July 2015, www.pressrepublican.com/news/local_news/after-attica-inmate-uprising-leads-to-reform/article_81cdfb7a-e03a-5e85-9161-4d6f183ef7b5.html.

him locked up, he could now effect change within his facility, or sometimes even the Department as a whole.

It didn't end there. Inmates were also granted the right to organize and elect prisoner representatives, men who could meet with the administration at regular intervals to discuss potential policy changes and the wants and needs of the convict collective. Today, this process within NYSDOCCS is known as the "Inmate Liaison Committee" or "ILC." Think of it as a union for inmates. Each member of the general population gets a vote, and each housing unit gets seats in a bizarre congress of criminality.

It was common to hear inmates plot openly about their various causes and grievances under this process. Some would file multiple complaints simultaneously, and, while rare, could even file against corrections personnel from previous facilities hundreds of miles away. Nothing energizes an inmate more than hearing about a fellow prisoner's legal situation. Eyes light up and suddenly cons become armchair lawyers.

Cons will offer their brothers behind bars free advice, help fill out forms, or aid each other in any way they can, all in the cause of their collective "justice." In reality, they mainly seek vengeance against officers or administrators for petty incidents, like enforcing an obscure policy that might cause a prisoner embarrassment. Sometimes these frivolous grievances actually went through, more often they did not. Still, wasting the administration's time via half-baked lawfare was only punished by rapid dismissal.

There's no punishment in place for filing false grievances. The resulting proliferation of bullshit leads to bureaucratic death by a thousand cuts. Since each grievance is expected to be taken seriously by correctional staff, any inmate can bog down the system in paperwork. This is even more pernicious if an inmate is "woke" enough to deploy key words that administrative personnel are trained to take more seriously than others. Words like "racism," "bigotry," and "safety and security" glow like torches to civilian staffers. The same goes for "religious rights," "dietary concerns," and "improper medication." Hell, all a black inmate has to do to get attention is accuse an officer of saying "nigger," regardless of any semblance of credibility.

Even though grievances usually fail to net inmates any real results, it doesn't dissuade them. They try...and try...and try again. Time is always on the side of the bitter felon. When you're locked up for eternity, you can afford to be as slow and methodical as necessary until achieving a doctorate in scheming. But when grievances fail, there's always recourse to play a more dangerous game. And that's when lawsuits enter the picture.

In NYSDOCCS, incarcerated criminals will typically (except for extreme circumstances) have access to what is called the "Law Library." They can use this State-provided resource to study legal books, prepare for lawfare, and ultimately sharpen their skills in order to bite the rotting system that binds them. The Law Library itself is an immense repository of information, and every correctional facility, by law, is equipped with one[16]. Aside from manuals, books, and extensive case law, they also feature typewriters, word processors, and even employ working legal clerks and notaries. There's also a seemingly limitless supply of ink ribbon and copy paper to lube the litigation machine. The Law Library empowers inmates (especially those of higher intelligence or agency than their dumber or lazier counterparts) to lash out against anyone they please at the State's expense.

In this endless conflict between inmates and prison, the system, in suicidal fashion, arms and supplies the enemy combatants with the tools to win not only battles but the war itself. This is the essence of jailhouse lawfare.

Inmates who are crafty enough to wage lawfare for personal gain (they are called "Legal Beagles" by other cons) cause a lot of trouble while incarcerated. Some are so good at lawyering that they can make a living of sorts by performing legal work for other inmates. While exchanging money is out of the question, a legal beagle can return to his cell after aping Atticus Finch to find it suddenly stocked with cigarettes, candy, treats, and even drugs. While this practice is strictly against Department rules, it's challenging to enforce. Unless a CO searches every piece of paper in a cell and reads every line of legal text therein, he might never catch on to an infraction at all.

In tandem with the Law Library, inmates also have access to free legal aid, all provided by outside organizations. Much like the muckety-mucks who provide inmates educational resources, these NGOs are typically run by liberal elite status-seekers or other progressive elements. While the organizations and their donors receive plenty of kudos from polite society, they do far more damage

---

[16]New York State, Corrections and Community Supervisions. "Law Libraries, Inmate Legal Assistance and Notary Public Services NO. 4483." 7 July 2020. https://doccs. ny.gov/system/files/documents/2020/11/4483.pdf

to society than their slick web sites would suggest.

One of the largest of these non-profit organizations in New York is Prisoner's Legal Services of New York, or PLS. Their mission statement is to "work tirelessly to fulfill its mission of providing high quality, effective legal representation and assistance to indigent prisoners, helping them to secure their civil and human rights and advocating for more humane prisons and for a more humane criminal justice system."[17]

While the wording might sound pretty and the cause may appear just, PLS and others like it do a great disservice. By providing "indigent prisoners" with free resources, materials, counsel, case-handlers, and a distributed newsletter called "Pro Se" (a rag often found in cells to cloak porno magazines or supply rolling papers) these do-gooders accelerate the decline of our civilization. They outfit thieves with the tools required to further rob the system from within its bowels. Organizations like PLS pervert our justice system and tip the scales of justice in favor of the guilty. Prison inmates have *already* had their days in court, but this *ex post facto* lawfare racket feeds their senses of entitlement and injustice, and often leads to inexplicable early releases.

With every legal victory a criminal achieves while incarcerated, the more generous the definition of "humane criminal justice system" becomes. It's an ice-tier slippery slope. Remember: at one time, inmates got bread and water. Today they receive interactive tablets and romps with their baby mamas on top of state resources to overturn their own convictions.

You may find my prison assessments illiberal, even antiquated and cruel. You may have heartstrings vulnerable to clichés of "inner-city youths" suffering as victims of "systemic racism." But after *living* the degeneracy of our prison system, I solemnly swear that prison is no longer true punishment for those sentenced there. If you are wronged by someone, and think incarceration serves justice on the offender, heed these words: You will not find justice via the American prison system. Prison will not deliver the punishment nor even the hard time you imagine. The thugs who rape daughters and kill wives? They get fat and happy in lockup while the liberal elite champion their rights and spit in victims' eyes. Our system is dying if not already dead. It elevates the criminal above the innocent, puts

---

17 "Prisoners' Legal Services Mission." *Prisoners Legal Services*, www.plsny.org/mission.html.

evil before good, and chaos over order.

This slow death is not sustainable. How long can this bloated, outdated, upside-down system continue to operate under the weight of such suicidal policies? My best guess: not very long. As long as NYSDOCCS and correctional departments across the United States continue to empower their wards while weakening themselves, their demise and replacement by an even more permissive crime-forgiving machine is a certainty. The public will continue to suffer at the hands of cowardly and corrupt politicians who find releasing and re-enfranchising felons to be better bets than "law and order." But who is to blame? Do you blame inmates for indulging in the buffet laid out before them? Do you blame pigs for feeding at the trough? Or do you blame the State for allowing *weakness* to grow and fester for decades in a core government function where *strength* is required above all else?

The answer speaks for itself.

Trying to find sanity and humanity in a member of the serious criminal class is insanity itself. The State has ceded its last vestiges of authority to the convicted criminals themselves. Correctional departments, and the politicians who operate them, conduct themselves like a group of gypsy puppeteers, turning their backs on the families of victims while opening flood gates for grievance, litigation, and rabble-rousing entitled convicts.

Enabled by lawfare, American criminals dealt a sickening blow to our correctional institutions. They enjoy lives behind bars far more luxurious than at any other point in human history, with the possible exception of Scandinavian prisoners. While cons in the United States may share the same status as those who were once gulagged in the Soviet Union, or locked away by 3rd world dictatorships in South America or Africa, any solidarity is merely symbolic. In reality, American prisoners live vastly more comfortably with access to more resources that someone in a Turkish jail could ever dream of. American prison as a deterrent to future crime is an abject fantasy. That era is long gone, replaced by flaccid rehabilitation and criminal appeasement.

This "fattening up" of the inmate and his civil liberties breeds an aura of invincibility and entitlement. Even if inmates fail to produce results via grievances or lawsuits, their damage is already done. They'll enjoy years to hone their craft and try again, repeatedly, until something sticks. In the age of lawfare, the criminal can win by attrition alone. It didn't have to be this way, but the State surrendered in the wake of Attica, and the criminals will have the last laugh.

13

NUTS AND BUTTS

How sexual depravity warps the mind of
incarcerated men...and how to solve it

"**1**:15 pm. CO McKraken on post for recreation. A/S: Sgt. Farris.
WC: LT Beauchamp. Fire and safety complete. Weapons set for
wall-tower storage. Yard tower safe and secure."

As I finished scrawling those words into the ragged logbook of
Yard Tower, I placed the cap back onto the tip of my ball point pen
and stuck it into the front of my uniform's shirt pocket. Warm spring
air wafted in through the windows of the tower after the weather had
turned a few weeks prior, and we were finally beginning to benefit
from the transition.

Yard Tower was one of my favorite posts. It was a safe, secluded
little strong point far above the vast expanse of the main yard, a big
grassy field filled with basketball courts, a baseball diamond, and a
football and soccer field where the inmates got to play year-round.
As long as they were outdoors, we had to be out there too, and Yard
Tower had to be manned and ready for any shenanigans. Despite my
lack of time, I had somehow managed to score a bid, which placed
me in that cushy spot at least twice a week. All I had to do was bring
the guns and ammo up six flights of stairs, hustle across the roof of
the facility, and lock myself in. After that, I had a relaxing couple of
hours all to myself and plenty of time to puff away at whichever cigar
was inside my humidor. Life in those moments was good.

Soon enough, the inmates began to file out into the yard, the
sound of their scuff-less Nikes and Timberlands echoing up from
below. When the yard was opened, it was usually a slow trickle at
first, as each inmate had to be searched and scanned before being
let outside. Sometimes it took up to fifteen minutes to process them
all, depending on the number who were set to come out; nicer days
guaranteed more inmates and shitty days guaranteed fewer. Since

that day happened to be a particularly nice one, there were quite a few.

Suddenly, the phone rang.

It was CO Panzetta from downstairs. He was the yard officer who watched the cons from the ground and held all the keys for the equipment boxes and bathroom stalls in the area. In his usual raspy, city accent, he cracked a joke about how much meat was in the yard. "Sixty-five," he remarked.

"Copy," I replied.

I wrote the number of inmates down in a separate entry in the logbook, making sure to leave a line of space for the Sergeant's entry. They were supposed to make regular rounds at certain times, so we would always leave a line open to sign the book if they were late. This ensured Sergeants and Lieutenants looked like they were where they were supposed to be, even when they were screwing around somewhere else. Low-level correctional cover-ups like this happened all the time, usually as a courtesy. But now that I look back on it? Fuck white shirts. They never did anything positive for officers, so there was no reason to cut them any slack when we never got any in return.

It wasn't long into yard time before I got a call from the opposite tower across the yard. My feet had already been kicked up onto the windowsill, and I was a quarter of the way through a Macanudo, so I was a little annoyed. I placed the smoldering stick on the ledge of the tower and answered the phone.

"McKraken. Yard Tower," I answered.

"Hobbs. Back Tower. Hey McKraken, look over at the soccer nets. See those two freaks? What the hell are they doing?"

"One sec."

I grabbed a pair of binoculars off of a small wooden desk inside the tower, brought them to my eyes, and surveyed the surface of the yard until I caught sight of two convicts. They were a pair of odd-looking whites. One was much older and had long, greasy, disheveled hair, while the other was younger and reminiscent of a Tolkienian goblin. He had a head shaved clean, and his face was taut with protruding bones. They were sitting Indian-style right at the base of the soccer nets; each had taken their shirts off and placed them in a neat clump on their respective laps.

"I see two cons sitting next to each other," I said, the old binoculars feeling rough against my eyelids. "Pretty close too."

"Yeah, I know. Look at the bald one. Where is his arm going?"

CO Hobbs replied.

"His arm? Well, one is on the grass and the other...holy shit!"

I couldn't believe my eyes. They were jerking each other off! Right there, in the middle of the yard, surrounded by sixty-three other inmates, and in broad daylight too. Each had his arm in the other's lap, using their shirts to cover their peckers as they did the deed. Naturally, I cringed.

"Hobbs, holy shit, they're jerking each other off, dude."

"Dude! I'll call the Sergeant. That's disgusting."

"You can say that again!" I replied.

"That's disgusting," he said again, this time with a laugh.

I sat back down in my high-backed chair and awaited further instructions. The Corrections Officer in me wanted to keep an eye on the situation at hand (no pun intended), but the disgusted human being in me wanted nothing more than to scream and claw my eyes out. Instead, I picked up the Macanudo and took a puff. It was a tasty smoke, but the cigar's phallic nature gave me a round of bad thoughts that turned me off to this particular tobacco tryst completely.

"Jesus Christ," I said to myself. "This place is fucked."

Then, the phone rang once more.

"McKraken. Yard Tower."

"McKraken, this is Sergeant Rob Garrison. How you doing there, buddy?"

"Good, Sarge. Did Hobbs tell you what's going on? I can confirm everything."

"Yes, he did. I'm coming out there with a team to bring these fuckers in and deal with them, okay? I need you to get the camera out of the locker and keep it rolling on the scene; just in case things get out of hand, we'll be covered. Think you can do that for me?"

"Yeah, no problem Sarge," I replied.

"Good! We'll be out there in a few." His words ended with a click of the phone.

I quickly went over to the tall locker near the tower's main door and unlocked it with a set of jingling keys. I opened it, removed a tripod and camcorder, attached the camera to the top of the tripod, focused, and before you knew it, I was filming the Yard like a blue-shirted Scorsese. Although he shot *Goodfellas*, I was shooting two fellas giving each other hand jobs.

Soon enough, Sergeant Rob Garrison came hustling outside, making a beeline towards the two degenerates. Sergeant Rob was a peculiar character and a longtime exemplar of day-shift hypocrisy in this particular facility. He had somehow managed to score a promotion to Sergeant after years of reading books, sleeping, and eating state mess hall food for years as an officer. Now that he was a white shirt, however, he would relentlessly bust the balls of any officer he caught doing the same things he did for years. As a result, he was universally loathed, and the name "*Big Blob* Garrison" was spoken behind closed doors every-time he happened to pass by.

As he trudged across the yard and up a grassy hill towards the soccer nets, his flabby form was flanked by a pair of older escort officers, each looking about as surly as you can get after being robbed of their usual mid-day naps. Dealing with a pair of sexual deviants engaging in homosexual behavior was not common for most COs, but despite their lack of experience, they came out with blue-colored rubber gloves on. Just in case.

And here I was, the big bad tower officer, keeping the viewfinder of his Sony handy-cam (no pun intended) directly on a pair of inmates who were furiously beating each other off on a glorious spring day. Once Big Blob and the Officers got close enough, the two handymen halted, but, by then, the psychological damage was already done. I was 29 years old and officially shooting gay prison pornography for the State of New York.

I'm not sure exactly what happened after that incident. I'm pretty sure those two soccer net sallies were removed from the facility for committing sexual acts. I remember Big Blob was hailed as a hero, albeit briefly, for "stopping crime." Hell, even the video itself (my very first and also last pornographic film), is probably saved somewhere on an SD card and stashed in an evidence locker in Albany.

If there was ever a time on the job that I was 100 percent certain about something, it was that I wanted to leave that job forever that day. And never look back.

* * *

State prison is about as dirty and debauched as the average human might imagine. It's a place where sexual degeneracy and desperation clash, and the resulting chemical reaction causes housing units and bathrooms to reek of ammonia and sweat. It's a place where decades-old smut magazines and jury-rigged picture books of other people's wives and girlfriends are openly traded for things as valuable as drugs or as cheap as snack cakes. It's a place where inmates will lock in the second a women's volleyball match starts playing on TV, and where female CO.s will fuck around with their porters in the back rooms of silent corridors.

It's not a big mystery why. When you take scores of high-testosterone members of the criminal class, pack them into a concrete bunker, and deny them the carnal pleasures they enjoyed while living free, you're bound to foster some degenerate shit. In NYSDOCCS, for instance, some inmates enjoy the privilege of sleeping with their wives on the weekends through the use of the Family Reunion Program.[18] It's one of the last vestiges of the idea of the "conjugal visit" in America. In addition to New York, only California, Connecticut, and Washington still allow the practice to continue. But not every guy gets the option. Conjugal visit programs typically require a stellar disciplinary record, and you can't just put any chicken-head or lot lizard down on the list and get it approved. Instead, the only way for most to get a nut off while incarcerated is to rely on pornography. And pornography always flows freely behind bars.

Tons of the stuff, from crusty old magazines to self-published smut literature and even self-made nudes done up by amateur sluts on the outside stock the prison cells of America's most secure lock-ups. It all resides there, festering in semen-coated stacks and abused by inmates for years on end. Eventually though, the same old porn stops working. Prisoners can only pleasure themselves to the same images and scenarios so many times before their dopamine-addled brain become numb to it. This, of course, triggers them to acquire new smut, new scenarios, and even explore new kinks and fetishes to satisfy the urge. In prison, a man will explore sexuality in ways he would never have considered if not for the presence of the most degenerate pornography there in the first place.

At first, it might only be pictures of tits and ass.

Then it might morph into 60 and over hardcore GILF porn and she-male mags.

Trust me, I've seen it first-hand. Young guys, old guys, and even hard, violent gang-bangers receive magazines from subscription companies on the outside. Usually it arrives in discreet manila

---

[18]Golden, Keith. "Family Reunion Program Offers a Pause in Prison Life." *Washington Square News*, 6 May 2018, nyunews.com/2018/04/30/family-reunion-program-offers-a-pause-in-prison-life/.

envelopes that COs deliver to the cells personally. Once opened, out drops a seventy page full-color porno rag filled with images of grandmas getting triple-teamed by hood blacks. Some of the most depraved, degenerate material you've ever seen will get shipped to a state convict, and the more time they have behind bars, the more disgusting the material will be. With our society's promotion of smut and sexual liberation through limitless internet porn, sex toys, and hook-up apps, one would think our free citizens would be more degenerate than those locked away from such "luxuries," but it's just not the case.

Evidence of this could be seen in some of the lifers and older inmates. These guys would keep encyclopedias of smut, new and old alike. Using cardboard from old cereal boxes and scotch tape, they would whip up customized books overflowing with their favorite starlets, poses, and pair-ups. "Pussy-books" they called them, and sometimes they'd even take them with them when transferred from jail to jail. Some of those pussy-books visited more state prisons than I did, and I was an employee!

But even porn, with its visceral brutality warping healthy sexual drives into cheap sadistic ephemeral fantasies, eventually becomes insufficient. Even the most hardcore erotica soon fails to titillate. Once that happens, and an inmate reaches the rock bottom of depravity, he begins to seek other ways to satisfy his cravings, even if it means going against his once-staunch morals and values. When that desperation hits a critical level, he will seek comfort and pleasure from other men. And in prison, the violent and non-violent alike so sometimes turn to homosexuality to continue the hunt for carnal satisfaction.

I'm talking about degenerate freaks, men whose minds have become so consumed by hunting for the next orgasm that they have wandered into parts unknown. They traverse the fine line between human and animal, and will engage in the most disgusting behavior imaginable just for a bit of pleasure and another dopamine hit. In one correctional facility, the officers and I encountered a new form of currency traded in the sex offender unit. They were called, "*grapes*," and were quite possibly the most revolting thing ever conceived.

The Grape was nothing more than the finger of a rubber or plastic disposable glove, usually found in mess halls for food service purposes. An inmate would masturbate into the glove and fill a finger up with his own semen. Upon completion, he would tie the finger off in a knot and remove it from the rest of the glove. What's left was a small, balloon-like, easily passable, and consumable unit of spunk that other inmates would trade for items like candy, smokes, and God knows what else. What the end-user of one of these grapes would do with such a vile product is left to your own imagination, but the demand was certainly there.

We appeared to hit the major distribution center for grapes on the housing unit during a routine cell-search one day, as we unwittingly stumbled across a re-purposed jar of peanut butter now half-filled with cum. The collective retching by security staff is remembered in that facility to this day.

Other inmates did indeed change their sexuality in order to achieve pleasure. While they might not consume human secretions sucked out from the rubber of a disposable glove, some would seek to get it directly from the source. Even though on the outside these inmates may have been straight, well-adjusted alpha males, after a long-enough incarceration they found themselves hunting booty or dick on the down-low. Sexual activity of any kind in a state prison is against the law, and violators receive severe disciplinary measures if caught. Yet prison provides ample opportunity for gay romps. Lusty enough inmates easily formed consensual relationships with fellow cons. Some even put on ostentatious displays of their newfound homosexuality, complete with feminine affects in their voices and limp, elegant hand gestures to complete the "booty-bandit" look.

But it's still uncommon.

In my years working in prisons, only once did I encounter homosexual behavior, that cursed day up in the guard tower. Gay stuff is frowned upon as degenerate and effeminate by convicts, and I agree wholeheartedly with them. But when these things *do* happen in a facility, and these relationships are discovered by the rest of the general population, they usually are a surprise to inmates and guards alike. The perpetrators are then typically mocked, shunned, isolated, and even assaulted for their "lifestyle choices." One openly-gay inmate (who was gay before entering prison and even had a same-sex marriage) was prevented from signing up for the FRP program with his husband. He was pressured by other convicts who were worried that the trailers (where the state provided the romper room beds) would become "unclean" with that "faggot shit."

That gay inmate technically had a right to a conjugal visit from his "husband"; the law didn't preclude it, and the opposition certainly didn't come from the COs. But instead of making a scene, he chose to play it safe and bend to the other convicts' will. He didn't want to become more of a target than he already was.

And that was smart.

But while openly gay relationships in prison are rare but real, there is an even rarer and more stereotypical sexual activity that also takes place. That, of course, would be prison rape. The Hollywood idea of lock-up as a vast gay anal rapehouse is a complete fabrication. While it does tragically occur from time to time, it's far less common than the public assumes.

The prison rape rarity is largely due to American criminal justice reforms. On September 4, 2003, the United States passed a federal law to stop the spread of rape and sexual assault in prisons and holding facilities across the country. The Prison Rape Elimination Act (PREA) set clear penalties for any sexual behavior by the incarcerated, consensual or otherwise.[19] It also provided inmates a host of treatment programs and therapy outlets if they had been victimized by sexual predators. All correctional staff, including nurses, officers, and administrators, are doggedly trained in the standards set by PREA, which has been remarkably effective in creating a zero-tolerance culture among prison staff for any sexual activity.

And that isn't an exaggeration. To demonstrate how seriously this issue was taken, officers were expected to carry a "PREA card" with them at all times, the contents of which broke down every step required to respond to rape or sexual assault. Supervisors would perform spot checks to ensure officers had the card on them, as if it were part of their uniforms. Failure to follow the bulleted list printed on the card, or failure to produce it when asked, could result in major trouble. Everyone, from the saltiest of old-timers to the youngest of new-jacks, thus took PREA stuff seriously. The PREA card was akin to Chairman Mao's "little red book," but since sexual assault incidents happened so rarely, the PREA card was just as rarely used. Mine collected dust in the back of my calendar book, and half the time, I forgot it was even there.

Ultimately though, there are still plenty of opportunities for horny convicts to do the deed. A homosexual inmate is much more willing to voluntarily give up his ass (or dick) rather than take someone else's by force. The latter option risks catching serious

---

[19] "Prison Rape Elimination Act." *National PREA Resource Center*, www.prearesourcecenter.org/about/prison-rape-elimination-act.

extra charges at double the effort. No man, not even the worst of the earth who inhabit these correctional facilities, deserves to be sexually abused against his will, and we must seek the complete abolishment of prison rape and the severest punishment for ALL sexual activity behind bars. Exceptions to this mercy would be made for child predators and rapists. These vile degenerates deserve only the worst our criminal justice system has to offer, and acts of vigilante justice against them by other convicts would only summon an indifferent yawn from me.

What more should be done about this pervasive if over-hyped problem? Man's carnal desires follow him wherever he goes, including long stretches in prison. We cannot cull those urges by force, absent castration. Still, we *can* work to prevent men from becoming the depraved, sex-addicted lunatics our current system enables, and in turn prevent rape and other degenerate behavior from proliferating behind bars.

I propose this: a complete banishment of pornography from the American prison system. Pornography has proven to be nothing but a slippery slope into absolute sexual depravity for the incarcerated man. If we remove it, a normal, healthy (heterosexual), and masculine ethos can thrive in its place.

Second, I propose the complete segregation of LGBTQ+ inmates from general populations. While we may not be able to change homosexual inclinations, we can prevent them from co-mingling with the heterosexual population. This would spare the straight and the gay from degeneracy that would not occur if not for the open and solicitous behavior from the homosexual inmate population. If an inmate self-identifies as gay prior to or during incarceration, or is caught engaging in homosexual acts, he would be immediately transferred to a homosexual unit, where he would be effectively quarantined from the heterosexual population.

Third, I propose a thorough re-examination of how we prosecute and sentence sexual abusers, rapists, and pedophiles. Our criminal justice system, especially in the State of New York, issues infuriatingly short sentences to convicted sexual offenders of every stripe. These light punishments do little to rehabilitate or reverse the damages these offenders impose upon our society. We have built a revolving door for sex offenders, who will leave the correctional system as quickly as they entered, determined to abuse innocent victims until they are caught again. During my time as a CO, I worked in a designated Sex Offender block. It was common to see the same faces file in and out repeatedly, almost always for breaking the parole terms or for committing the same crimes that got them locked up in the first place. Instead, I would mandate much longer sentences for all sexual offenders, with additional penalties for any sexual offenses while incarcerated. And yes, I would mandate chemical castration for the worst repeat offenders (i.e., pedophiles) to spare the most vulnerable in society from further torture at their hands.

With these proposed reforms, our correctional institutions would better protect the public as well as the inmates. Their purpose is not to be unfairly punitive, nor to subject anyone to "cruel and unusual punishment," nor to enact a macabre vengeance upon degenerates. If anything, these reforms are morally righteous. A majority of Americans would agree with them if asked in a private setting with a guarantee of anonymity.

These reforms would provide the incarcerated man a way forward—a means to overcome and truly make amends for wrongs committed. By denying access to pornography, we would prevent the addictive and destructive spiral into degeneracy. To segregate the afflicted from the still-decent would at least slow the spread of the rot. And by punishing those who succumb to depravity, we would deter many other prison house pathologies as well.

But it starts with a ban on pornography: ending the glut of smut. We theoretically punish prior crimes in our prisons, while turning a blind eye to many sins within them. We have to be unapologetic about such stern measures. Until then, inmates will continue to eat *grapes* and play handball under soccer nets, and officers like me will be forced to film it.

14

GANGSTER

How unions wage impotent war and keep
good men engaged in futility

The Desmond Hotel was a beautiful place in Albany, NY, located a convenient quarter-mile from the city's international airport. Built in the 1970s as the area's only upscale hotel and conference center, The Desmond Hotel still stands as a piece of Americana. The first time I walked through its doors, I was filled with a sense of awe at the venue's "colonial village" decor. Large courtyards within the grounds were decorated in a kind of Revolutionary War town square aesthetic, complete with imitation storefronts, bubbling fountains, and lamp posts glowing with amber light. Staying at the Desmond instilled a warm, patriotic feeling. And the feeling lingered long after leaving its cozy interior. It was a classy joint, and for a blue-collar hack who could barely make car payments and spent more money on chicken wings and video games than he ever did on anything productive, I felt a little out of place.

But what brought me to the Desmond was not the glowing reviews, nor the need for rest after a long night on the road. In fact, my opinion of Albany was so low, it was among the last places you would catch a man like me. Instead, on a cold March afternoon a few years ago, I found myself enjoying this fine establishment for one reason: The Executive Assembly.

Known as the EA, this was the bi-monthly meeting of the minds of the New York State Correctional Officers and Police Benevolent Association or NYSCOPBA. In layman's terms, it was the prison guard union, and anybody who was anybody in the world of New York State Correctional Officers made sure to attend. At the time, I had just begun to consider running for Steward of my local sector. My dad had been involved in the union as an operating engineer down in Manhattan for years. Hearing him speak highly of it instilled a pro-working class mentality in me, even as a youngster.

After seeing him get mixed up in strikes and meetings and fighting the good fight many years ago, I figured I'd give it a shot now that I was a working-class stiff just like him. The vote was right around the corner, and before I threw my name in the ring, I wanted to know what being a Steward was *actually* like. And there was no better way to do that than to attend the Executive Assembly at the Desmond and get a peek into the inner workings of it all. The politics. The arguments. The motions and the struggles! I wanted to champion the working man and make a difference in the world, not only for myself but also for my correctional brothers and sisters.

I was energized, excited, and anxious to get started.

So I asked the local union chiefs if I could attend, and they agreed to let me accompany them to the EA as a guest. They were eager to breathe new life into the union, and show young-bloods like me what the business was all about. They considered it a "passing of the baton" (pun intended), and wanted to empower new jacks who pursued the membership's best interests.

One of the chiefs was a CO named Mancuso. He was a squat Italian with slick black hair and the eyes of a shark. He spoke loudly, smiled constantly, and didn't understand the concept of personal space. But it didn't matter; he had a heart as big as the Desmond itself, and always acted with a profound sense of responsibility.

The other chief was a CO named Zunino. He shared his counterpart's big smile, Italian ancestry, and shiny black hair, but while Mancuso was a doer, Zunino was a talker. He was a big political guy; he talked up a storm and was a master of rumors and the art of cultivating information for (and sometimes against) individuals. While he had good intentions for the union, you always got the vibe that he expected more. He had ambition. Drive. He wanted to move and shake with the movers and shakers, and if he had to fight in the trenches as a soldier for some small-time sector as a Chief or Treasurer just for a shot at greatness in the Executive Board someday, he'd fight as hard as he could.

Between Zunino's skullduggery and Mancuso's genuine likability, you had a pretty strong team that could battle workplace injustices across the spectrum. There was just one problem. Zunino and Mancuso hated the Executive Board, and the Executive Board hated them right back.

As I walked through The Desmond's village square courtyards, taking in the 1700's aesthetics and passing throngs of union men on their way to the luncheon buffet, I got a ring on my cell that was just loud enough to break through my trance and bring me back to reality. It was a text from Mancuso.

"Hey buddy! When u get in, we're in room 107. Got something for u!"

I found room 107 after a bit of navigating, knocked on the door, and it opened shortly thereafter.

"Hey, buddy, how you doing? How was the trip?" asked Zunino, his hairy arms crossed as he hovered over one of the room's two full-sized mattresses. Much like the corridors and courtyards, the rooms were equally impressive and imbued with colonial spirit.

"Good, thanks. When's the meeting start?" I asked, eager to see the union in action. I had just driven about an hour and a half to reach this hotel, and I didn't want the trip to go to waste.

"In like two hours. We're going to hit the buffet first, and then we conduct business. But hey, check these out!"

Mancuso emerged from the back of the room with a big cardboard box. He carried it over to one of the beds and plopped it down with a bounce. With his usual, mischievous grin, he ripped the top of the box open with his bare hands, reached inside, and pulled out a single bright red t-shirt. On the front was an American Flag right above the breast, but on the back was "Make D.O.C.S. Great Again" printed in bold white font.

"Wow," I replied. "That's some t-shirt."

"Like it, buddy? Hahaha!" Mancuso cackled like a madman as he slipped the shirt on over his polo. "We got a whole box of 'em made out-of-pocket, and we're gonna hand 'em out to the other stewards who're pissed off at the Executive Board! It's gonna be gangster! Here! Take one."

Mancuso threw me an extra-large. He knew my size with a glance, but I had no intention of wearing it. This was my first introduction to NYSCOPBA and its officials. I damn sure didn't have open rebellion against the current executive board on my list of things to do during my first EA. So I graciously bowed out of their symbolic protest. Maybe next time, I promised them, and they understood.

We ate a catered lunch and made a few rounds of introductions with the chiefs from other sectors before receiving word that the meeting was about to start. Mancuso and Zunino had managed to hand out about twenty or thirty shirts to guys with similar bones to pick with the executive board. The caveat was that if they wore them to the meeting, the shirts were free. If not, there was a $20 charge per shirt. So far as I know, they didn't make any sales.

But for every shirt they gave out, there were about a dozen or so union men who eyed us with contempt. I had never been in a place like this, and already I was making enemies purely by association. It wasn't very pleasant, but I was loyal to these two men who took me under their wing. While I wasn't aware of all of the political intrigues going on around me, I was open to learning more.

After lunch we shuffled our way inside the main conference room, a large chamber filled with folding chairs and tables that the chiefs would use to take notes, sip on soft drinks, and watch as the Executive Board at the front of the room conducted the meeting. Guests like myself didn't get a seat at any table, so I made do with a chair off to the side with the rest of the unelected membership. I sat next to a few guys from Wallkill Correctional Facility, and before long the meeting commenced and the board took center stage.

As I sat and watched business unfold, I got to see a few exciting things. From prisons as far north as Clinton and Watertown and as west as Attica and Auburn, stewards from across the state discussed the various ongoing issues in those regions. As the executives spoke and passed on new information to the stewards, the stewards freely lined up at a microphone in the center of the room to ask questions or voice concerns. The board addressed them one by one, creating a sort of assembly line of dialogue. The whole process was surprisingly interesting, and I was pumped to witness "democracy in action" and learn how the unions *actually* operated.

It was a good, positive experience. Then Zunino took the mic.

"Officer Zunino. Chief from [REDACTED] correctional facility," he said, speaking as slowly and deliberately as he could manage. There was a sly look about him that revealed more than any words. In his mind he was looking up at the enemy, and the enemy was looking right back at him. "During the last EA meeting, you fine gentlemen of the board told the membership that 10,000 dollars were going to be allocated for the continuation of pro-correctional officer television ads placed on local networks across the state. My question to you, Mr. President, is: Where are these advertisements? Who is seeing these advertisements?"

The room was quiet, save from some grumblings of support from the stewards who were wearing "Make D.O.C.S. Great Again" t-shirts. It was common to see a chief walk up to the mic with the sole intention of poking the bear. However, Zunino remained one of the few with the balls to do it regularly, and in doing so, he had earned quite the reputation for being a "shit-stirrer" and acting "gangster" on the mic. His way of calling the executives out on every little move they made, and every talking point they manufactured, created a certain tension in NYSCOPBA. The pair of chiefs who took me under their wing openly relished the reputation.

"Well, hold on, Zunino. Let me clarify. Jim, can I gate a date on that?" replied the President. He was a man as tall and wide as you would expect in a correctional officer, but he had ditched his state uniform and a post on a housing unit for a Nautica suit and this office job. His eyes almost rolled out of his head as he saw Zunino walk up, instinctively preparing himself for the curve-ball about to be pitched.

"January 25th, Mike," replied the Parliamentarian, a thin, balding paper-pusher hired to keep things orderly and consistent with Robert's Rules. He shuffled some papers with trembling hands and sweat beading on his pock-marked brow.

"So during the last EA meeting, we voted on a motion to run additional television ads to counter the anti-union rhetoric coming from Albany and the Governor's office. And, yes, Zunino, you would be correct in that amount of $10,000."

There was another round of grumbling across the conference hall, this time louder and much more widespread. Was the executive board caught with their pants down? Did they really mismanage money and renege on a stated promise? Zunino smirked and pressed closer to the mic.

"Then it looks like the executive board has some explaining to do. Why was the money not spent on those additional commercials? Why does the treasurer's report show no money allocated to the media team when the Governor is out there every day, blaming us for the State's problems?"

The room was now at a simmer. Mancuso was grinning like a hyena, and every man in Zunino's camp was itching for a win. The President, although challenged, didn't flinch. Instead, he took a sip of cold water with a steady grip, cleared his throat, and knocked Zunino's curve-ball straight out of the park.

"Well, let's be clear here. We *did* vote to pay for more commercials. However, that was under the stipulation that the money was only to be used pending the results of the ongoing contract negotiations. If the Governor agreed to sit with the collective bargaining committee, we would forgo the commercials altogether. As of last week, the Governor agreed. So no new commercials will be released for the time being. Sorry if there was a miscommunication, Zunino, but that stipulation was on the vote."

Zunino's face morphed from confident to annoyed. The collected stewardship's opinion was bouncing back and forth quicker than a game of ping pong, and I found myself struggling to predict the winner of this particular match. Instead, I sat back and sipped on my fifth Diet Coke, courtesy of the Desmond catering team.

"Sorry?" Zunino barked through the mic. The room was now still with silence, and many, especially those who wanted to see the executive board get verbally eviscerated, sat at the edge of their seats. "All we get is a sorry? That stipulation was never mentioned to the membership! Whatever happened to accountability?"

"Right...Well, Zunino, the stipulation was always there; in fact, it was printed on the motion itself, right there on line twelve of paragraph three. I, as president of the executive board, personally apologize to you, Zunino, if this wasn't communicated more clearly. Still, everything about this is above board," the President shot back, eyeing his counterpart with a sharp, eagle-eyed glare. Better men had stepped to the mic to battle with this particular union official, and better men had failed. Now, Zunino was visibly shaken. The peanut gallery's opinion had shifted against him once more, and he was now reeling from the sting of politics: the cruel and merciless swing of a pendulum the President now held firmly.

However, what came next was one of the most far-out, ridiculous things I had ever heard a grown man say in a public setting.

"Sorry? All we get is a sorry? *Well, we killed the Jews, but that doesn't make it right!*"

Suddenly, the room exploded in a loud cacophony of "oohs" and horrified exasperated gasps. I almost shot six ounces of caffeinated soda out of my nose as I heard the words come out of Zunino's mouth. Not only did his comparison of the issues at hand not make any sense, but it also served to shock and petrify all of the other more politically correct individuals within the room.

About five or six stewards rushed to line up behind the mic in the wake of his blunder, awaiting their turn to speak. The groans and gossip grew to a roaring thunder all across the conference hall, and even the president himself looked frazzled. God forbid this should get out to the wrong people, and he would take flak from the ADL or SPLC for allowing anti-Semites within his stewardship. He had a right to be alarmed too; the union lawyer, a man named "Goldman," sat three chars away with a look upon his face like he had just been victimized in a ruthless pogrom. While Zunino may not have been exactly "anti-Semitic," it certainly was anti-sanity. Instead, he simply shrugged his shoulders and frowned as if to say, "What's wrong?"

Order was restored after a few minutes, but only after a round of begging from the executive board. A dozen or so stewards marched to the mic during the chaos. They all used their time to firmly denounce Zunino and even having his comments struck from the official record. By now, a lot of the red t-shirts were coming off, save for a few die-hard Zunino supporters. As for me? I hung my head in embarrassment.

My first time witnessing an Executive Assembly meeting, and already it was a complete, unmitigated shit show. And for what?

For nothing.

But if there was anything positive to take from that meeting for an uninitiated union hopeful like myself, it was the education. I had witnessed first-hand what life within NYSCOPBA was like. I didn't learn any of the hard-hitting, gritty union politicking as I had hoped, nor was it an informative course on the intricacies of Robert's Rules of Order. Instead, it served as a grim foreshadowing, a stark indicator of things to come.

A monument to the fruitlessness of the current order, and I stood before it. Thunderstruck.

* * *

In corrections, a significant portion of the average shift is dedicated to absolutely nothing. If I had to guess, I'd say roughly 90% is complete stone-cold oblivion. Now, out of that 90%, 10% is comprised of walking to and from areas, 10% of it is eating, and the rest? Well, that leaves about 70% of an 8-hour shift devoted to either staring at inmates quietly to observe their actions or talking with other officers in the vicinity. If you're lucky enough to be working a post where the latter is an option, then guess what? Chances are you're going to be complaining.

A lot.

Corrections Officers love to bitch. They love to moan and wheeze about the slightest things, from minor changes in their regular monotonous day to the nation's politics writ large.

Whenever a Corrections Officer runs out of things to bitch about, he will go so far as to manufacture issues to keep the bitching rolling. A rumor spread against a fellow CO, for example, or maybe even whipping out a directives manual and reading until seeing something to bitch about. As a rule, the easier it is to work a post or facility, the greater and louder the bitching becomes.

Sometimes all of this complaining will bubble over to the point where it's no longer adequate. The talk becomes a serious issue, and a great clamor for action rips across the facility until things change for the better.

That's where the union comes in—acting as an intermediary between the blue shirts and the white ones. It has the express purpose of advocating for changes until they are enacted in the workplace. All it takes is a few good men willing to run for Steward. While the job comes with some nice perks, it also brings the heavy burden of responsibility. Once elected, these men become receptacles for the woes and complaints of all of their brothers and sisters. Every action (or inaction) is examined under an electron microscope. If they fail to deliver results or serve as the bearer of bad news, they become the focus of bitching themselves.

It happened to me.

In early autumn of 2017, I ran for my local union sector, and to my surprise, I won. I was happy about it too, not because I was seeking special privileges or political gain, but because I had a unique fascination with unions and workers' rights in general. I *actually* wanted to do good by the working class. I wanted to learn. I wanted to make positive changes. I wanted to fight the administration tooth and nail, an administration that was becoming more tyrannical as the years went on.

Well, I got my wish. I was now one of these bitching receptacles, and due to my IQ being two or three points above the average microwave oven, the chief selected me to serve as Recording Secretary. While still a steward, the secretary was more or less a bookkeeper, a man in charge of keeping minutes of every meeting and producing notes, memos, and keeping track of all of the votes and motions made in such meetings. It was an excellent place for me. I could use the experience to sink my teeth into some of the pressing issues of the day while also figuring out union business at a pace that I was comfortable with.

While my hopes were high, I soon discovered the bitter truth: that the union, and NYSCOPBA in general, created more divides than it was bridging. The longer I served in a union capacity, the more I reflected on the ridiculous spectacle that was my first Executive Assembly meeting, and the more I kicked myself for believing that grand posturing I witnessed between chiefs and those in power was just an anomaly.

In reality, the union itself was nothing but a charade, an ineffective organization that offered little unity and even fewer results. While NYSCOPBA operates statewide and addresses issues and grievances from officers at the local, regional, and statewide levels, it fails to win any meaningful victories against those it squares off against. Much like the department itself, the union apparatus is broken, and rarely, if ever, does it procure the wins that officers *actually* want, even the easiest ones to achieve! Most often a team of elected stewards and executives merely pander to the local membership long enough to gain their support before an election. Once seated, they work at a snail's pace or ignore the issues altogether.

Instead of fighting the administration, local chiefs instead direct their time and energy into hobnobbing and working *with* the administration to forge half-baked compromises. And those compromises almost always work in favor of the brass. This in turn creates a dynamic whereby officers continually receive nothing substantial from their labor-management meetings or grievances, and the brass, while not total in their domination, still inch closer toward their goals with no chance of that inch ever being reversed. I frequently witnessed this spineless behavior up close. Despite several instances in which an entire facility practically begged for a specific policy change, the stewards would instead prostrate themselves toward their superiors, and then grow resentful toward the membership they swore to serve!

"Management has a right to manage," they would say as they returned to the housing units out back with their heads hung in shame. "You get more flies with honey than with vinegar!"

Pathetic.

The "union," it turns out, is nothing but a popularity contest. Elected stewards and chiefs are the most friendly, likable members of the officer staff, voted in by inner circles of best friends, good old boys, and others who bowed to peer pressure. Once they gain the title, it becomes a mark of prestige, and they walk around a facility spouting long platitudes about their moral superiority and how hard they're fighting in the trenches for officer "rights."

But behind the scenes, things are quite different. Chiefs and other stewards regularly badmouth "problem officers" for causing trouble or for filing too many grievances with the system. They praise the administration for "how nice they are" or "how good *this* superintendent is compared to the *last* one." They belittle officers for being "entitled" and not knowing how well they have it compared to other facilities in the region. As a result, stewards and chiefs never actually improve in the job. Instead, they get better in their ability to come up with different excuses for shortcomings or manufacture different deflection techniques to place blame back onto those who spoke up for themselves.

This counter-productive and lackadaisical view of employee concerns resonates from the union's lowest levels to its very upper echelons. In a way, it serves as a direct mirror of the Department of Corrections itself, with its hired personnel skirting responsibility whenever possible and only ever engaging with unavoidable business. While the Executive Board of NYSCOPBA is responsible for policy and clerical minutiae from their offices in Albany, and the organization does provide legal resources to officers under disciplinary review or dispute, it does little when it comes to more significant, system-wide problems. It never reverses any of the state's most tyrannical policies, and it never changes the culture of corrections in favor of the working man. Whatever small victories they do achieve are minuscule and virtually worthless.

During my time as a Corrections Officer, almost all of it was spent working without a contract. This means that *for years* the State and NYSCOPBA were in a collective bargaining session and couldn't reach agreement on pay raises and benefits that reflected the needs of the membership. While this may seem like a good thing, with officers and the union refusing to accept peanuts from the State, in reality, the entire fight was meaningless. After years of stalling and refusing the State's offers (which were, quite frankly, insulting[20]), the union caved and advocated for the latest offer to come to a vote, knowing full well the deal was abysmal.

The membership, torn over the details, cast their ballots, and the deal was ultimately accepted. We were now entitled to years of back pay issued via a heavily-taxed retroactive check, a low percentage five-year raise that didn't even match inflation, and a

---

[20]"Security Services Unit (SSU) - 01 and 21." *Governor's Office of Employee Relations*, goer.ny.gov/security-services-unit-ssu-01-and-21.

hike in our medical co-pays. If the union had prevented this offer from being voted on by the membership, such a garbage contract would never have come to pass! Instead, given the chance, the membership accepted crumbs.

But why would working-class men and women affirm such a terrible contract? Simply put, greed. Many of the stewards, chiefs, and the officers they represented hailed from the northern and western parts of the State and the minority-laden south. Workers in those regions were drooling for years for any extra money whatsoever. With a lower standard of living than those in the central areas of New York, these men and women were hungry for the retro check—any retro check. They were readily willing to sell out the rest of the membership for a down payment on a new boat, motorcycle, truck, or fully loaded sedan.

Union strong!

Meanwhile, as the contract circus finally wrapped up and ended in a pitiful whimper, our liberties continued to deteriorate. More and more progressive, anti-officer policies were pushed, and our personal spaces (including bodies) were searched and violated in wide-sweeping, no-warning raids from the State's in-house investigation teams. By the end of my career, Corrections Officers— proud members of the law enforcement community—were viewed with more scrutiny than the convicts.

But where were NYSCOPBA and the executive board during all of this? They were barely seen or heard, only ever providing token responses and canned statements in opposition to the State's tyranny, but never willing to fight it in any meaningful way. They reminded me of the Republican Party. Every once in a while they would conduct an "educational picket" where officers would be allowed during off-hours to stand around a public space near one of the prisons and hold signs and scream at oncoming traffic. These pitiful imitations of actual strikes did little but fuel our impotent rage and earn small news stories on the local networks, all of which morphed into hit pieces by the end of the segments.[21]

To be clear: are there good union men in civil service unions like NYSCOPBA? Yes. There's a lot of well-meaning people eager to make a difference. Hell, I was one of them, and I worked with many other

---

[21]"Correction Officers Picket to Call Awareness to Violence." *Spectrumlocalnews.com*, spectrumlocalnews.com/nys/rochester/news/2016/05/25/correction-officers-picket -to-call-awareness-to-violence.

really good ones, too. But the sad reality is that these good men are so few and far between that many of them get disillusioned or lost in the shuffle. They are drowned out by a sea of loudmouths and personalities and are too few to be heard. Sometimes they are corrupted by the allure of working in Albany, away from the misery of the prisons themselves. Those elected to serve on the Executive Board work full-time in a union capacity, and even keep a spot back at the prison they came from. This is such a powerful allure for some chiefs and stewards that they will work in smaller positions for the promise of eventual promotion, officer issues be damned.

Although the union is the only outlet for a Corrections Officer to address concerns, it nevertheless stands as an obstacle to any redress of grievances. Think of it as a giant pressure release valve: it operates purely to funnel the determination and energy of upstanding men and women into an outlet that sets them up for total failure. Instead of those individuals going boldly forth to fight for justice in their workplace by creating solidarity and righteous rage among their coworkers against unjust policies, the union caps them off at the knee, miring them in unnecessary politics and toothless avenues of attack. The protesting officer holds his head in frustration as the chiefs convince him he is wrong for wanting change. He grows weary as his union meetings dissolve into veritable drunken fistfights over secondary issues. He fills with fury as he is issued a serf's contract that does nothing but serve the interests of the State.

Anyone who might prove to be an *actual* defender of worker's rights within the Department of Corrections and Community Supervision is essentially muzzled. It's an insidious trap, and it works quite well. Instead of unity in the union, one only finds chaos. Instead of trust, one only finds deception. Instead of success, one only finds failure. And the State and its many administrations and executives watch with gleeful eyes and laugh their way to a cushy retirement. Expecting unions like these to provide results is absolutely soul-crushing. But why does it have to be this way? What could have possibly led to the toothless, ineffectual labor union we have now?

While I cannot speak for other states, New York effectively turned public sector unions like NYSCOPBA into effeminate geldings via the Public Employees Fair Employment Act, or "Taylor

Law."[22] This piece of legislation, passed in 1967, provides a voice for civil service unions within the State but also makes strikes by these organizations illegal. Hefty fines or even jail time can be dealt to union members or officials who even talk about a strike to fellow members. Officers and stewards are thus predictably petrified of even mentioning the idea.

The fines themselves are as follows: for every day you strike, you lose two days' pay. Strikes can even cost the union its "Dues Check-off" system, which places dues collection in the State's hands and makes it an automatic deduction from all New York public employees. To lose that system would force a union like NYSCOPBA to manually collect dues from every member, passing the helmet around like on a construction site until everyone pays up. This would make the union coffers a little lighter to say the least, given the sheer number of workers NYSCOPBA employs.

The other penalties, while severe, are not insurmountable. If the price for workers' rights and the preservation of justice in an increasingly insane society is a lighter paycheck and maybe a few days in the clink, then I'd say the price is fair. In this world, meaningful change always results from action, not from words. Corrections, if it is a livelihood to be maintained and improved for the white working-class (the predominant component of the profession,) cannot rely solely on negotiations and parlays with the State led by self-interested cowards.

The State itself, run by duplicitous vampires who want nothing more than to demean and demoralize its taxpayers, has only its agendas, elections, and bottom line at heart. Instead, workers must collectively give a resounding "no" to these creatures at every opportunity, and only say yes when our demands are met. We cannot budge, we cannot break, we cannot just turn our backs on these urbanite pseudo-intellectuals who puppeteer this sick society unless we do so from a position that gives us a chance at total victory.

Of course, this level of defiance will require action and courage and tenacity from men willing to take a stand regardless of the consequences. Simply put: To save corrections, Corrections Officers need to strike. Taylor Law be damned.

Workers must picket, day in and day out, until they win the

[22] "New York State Public Employees' Fair Employment Act - The Taylor Law." *Governor's Office of Employee Relations*, goer.ny.gov/new-york-state-public-employees-fair-employment-act-taylor-law.

State's grudging respect, which has been absent for a long time. Corrections is a fragile machine that requires lots of manpower to keep all of its insane programs and policies running as intended. Behind every inmate college class, behind every conjugal visit trailer, behind every close visitation room, fully catered religious event and every sex change operation performed on a transsexual predator, a Corrections Officer is required to man that ridiculous post. Deny the state access to that manpower, and watch with a smile as the entire progressive system collapses under the weight of its own pathological altruism. They would beg us to come back and offer us gold bullion for the privilege.

But what of the old-timers? What of the older family men? What of the officers addicted to overtime who never make a union meeting unless scheduled on a day that they work and ONLY if they serve pizza? If you're a Corrections Officer and find yourself beset by these kinds of men, you must be wary around them. They are the weak, ineffectual paycheck addicts who oversaw the decline of corrections into a kind of cuckoo clock, much as the Boomers presided over a once-great nation transformed into a trans-continental insane asylum.

"It'll never work!" they'll shout. "I've got a truck payment and kids to feed! I don't have time to strike!"

Again, pathetic. While these vermin fill your ears with poison and beg you to join in their complacency, the enemy (i.e., the State) only gets stronger, and your situation weaker. You'll know them when you see them, typically older men with salt and pepper beards who have "seniority" over you, and you might even look to them for workplace knowledge and practical on-the-job advice. While wise, they are at core fearful men who have grown fat, happy, and accustomed to the piddling crumbs given to them by the administration. They have no desire to rock the boat in the twilight hours of their career, and as a result, they are useless. They offer all those who share a thirst for justice and righteous reform nothing of value. These people are nothing but dead weight to the cause, and even scabs in service of the system.

It's incredible how a man can cower when his fragile world is threatened. Boil him down and you will find only fear, not just of the barbed hand that feeds him, but also of greatness and the heights that could be achieved if only he clenched his jaw and raised his fist in defiance. Those who find themselves in positions of rightful revolt shouldn't be afraid at all! They should feel enlightened. They should feel hopeful! If we, as working men, had the power to topple these oppressive workplace regimes through a unified wildcat strike, then these odious laws, restrictions, and bills wouldn't have passed to begin with. If anything, the regime penalizes us and establishes barriers to strikes because of how much they fear us using it to better ourselves!

Ultimately, no good comes from passivity. No change comes from inaction. My advice may derive from a corrections mindset, but it applies to any cause or workplace reeling under the tightening grip of "progress." If you, a police officer, or teacher, or transit worker, or any civil public employee for that matter are mistreated by workplace policies or agendas and feel disillusioned by your union's inability or unwillingness to combat them, you must strike!

You must not only strike, but you must also become familiar and comfortable with the idea of striking, and you must do so with or without your current union's assistance or approval. Unions can grow just as complacent and useless as the laziest worker in your membership, and if you cannot rely on your representatives to grow a spine, you must abandon them for your sake and the well-being of your brothers. You cannot rely on laws being changed to make it easier for you to advance your interests; you cannot rely on your union to bring you victories. The only thing you can rely on your union to do is to bring home failures and continue to operate as a pressure release valve for the rage of righteous men. Trust in union leadership is a fool's errand.

Ignore the nay-sayers, muckrakers, and cults of personality.

Ignore the threats from management and government politicians.

Ignore the groans of the lazy, complacent, and treacherous.

Set aside all the bickering and *strike*. For if you don't, your situation will only grow so unbearable you will resign or take early retirement, dooming those who come after you to a life in service to the liberal altar growing more demonic every year.

You need to feel the sting of sacrifice before you can reap the rewards of victory.

You need to *stop* "livin' the dream."

You need to *start* riding the tiger.

15

SHIT IN THE WOUND

*A window into the world of prison medicine
and how badly it's abused by humanity's worst*

If you've ever been inside one prison infirmary, you know what every prison infirmary is like. The gleaming floor tiles. The white fluorescent lights. The overwhelming scent of disinfectant hitting your nose like a sledgehammer the second you walk in. They are usually outfitted with air conditioning, clean beds, and flat-screen televisions, like little windows into a world that once was for the incarcerated man. So close to home, yet so far out of reach.

I was working the infirmary post one afternoon at a maximum security facility, and the keys lay heavy at my waist. While the shift had only just begun, I already felt like it had been dragging for hours. Something about walking into the front doors of a state prison always managed to sap my energy, no matter how many hours I slept or how much coffee I gulped. My partner, a young, lean, brown-haired Pollack named Duran, had the logbook that day, and I had the escort. We took turns making regular rounds on the unit between the two of us, and took our time making the hardest decision we had all night: what to watch on TV.

But before we could debate the fine particulars of Wednesday night programming, we had to do a round. You never knew if the day-shift guys actually did their job or if they just wrote in the book that they did, so you remedied that by doing a round the second you got to your post to make sure everything was okay. Since on paper *all* of the rounds were technically my job, I took the first one. I unlocked the heavy metal bars which led into the medical gallery, and prepared to inspect some live, breathing bodies.

"Oh, one second! I'm almost ready!" A soft voice echoed from behind me in sing-song fashion. It came from the nurse's station, a small area in the infirmary set aside for civilian nurses to prepare med carts and fill out paperwork safely and away from the prying eyes of convicts. The nurses on duty were always changing in and out; the turnover rate on prison civilians was understandably high, so we got used to seeing new faces all the time. I hadn't seen this particular nurse before today, and she was a complete smoke show: a short, older woman with long blonde hair and who could wear a bland set of scrubs and a pair of white Keds like a teenager's TikTok fantasy. She had a name-tag on her ample chest which read, "Nurse Foster."

"Sorry, I had no idea you guys just came on shift! Almost done!"

"No problem!" I shot back, holding the heavy door open wide and smiling. "I didn't see you there either, so I guess that makes two of us."

She hurried along in a frantic display that came across as cute, filling her cart with all the necessary medication she needed to dispense, each in little brown bags, one for each admitted inmate. The nurses usually made a medication run around this time; she just happened to be a bit early. Before long, she followed me into the corridor. I locked the gate behind us, and off we went.

This particular infirmary wasn't large. It had two small wards filled with beds that inmates shared on one end. These wards were bare-bones when it came to accouterments, and didn't have any televisions or phone access until certain times of the day. The rest of the infirmary was composed of isolation beds, which are single inmate chambers that locked securely and provided medical staff the control they needed to monitor inmates with severe injuries or ailments. As Nurse Foster and I walked the corridor, she spun tales of all the other prisons she used to work before she landed here. I obliged with stories of my own; it was a ritual that civilians and officers often engaged in, a kind of prison small-talk. Then we suddenly stopped, and the casual banter took a dark turn.

"Okay, so this patient coming up is a little... special," she whispered, clearly masking her preferred choice of words. "You might want to hold your nose; it's not going to be very pleasant."

I felt my chest tighten up. Prison already stunk pretty bad, and if a nurse was complaining about the odors, you knew something had to be seriously wrong. I walked over to the door leading to ISO bed Number 5. I unlocked the first door with a thick, steel bit key, turned the lock, and swung it open. The nurse followed me inside with her cart, and I unlocked a second door, swinging it open and allowing Nurse Foster to head inside. She positively beamed with energy and goodwill as she spoke with a bedridden inmate across the room. I turned my gaze toward the convict, and with every ounce of strength I could muster, I resisted the urge to vomit from the sights and smells.

On the surface of a modern hospital bed lay a greasy, shaggy-haired convict wearing a pair of thick, coke bottle glasses. He sported an unkempt mustache and barely looked at us as we entered his dark domain. He gripped a long remote control that he used to furiously change channels on his personal widescreen television that hung on the wall with heavy-duty bolts. The putrid smell wafting from his body was unlike anything I had ever experienced: a ghoulish blend of feces, body odor, and necrotic flesh. Without flinching, Nurse Foster marched over to the inmate, a man I later learned went by Gonzalez, and produced a tube of antibiotic cream.

As she approached, Gonzalez nodded, grinned, and grunted in an abrupt, primal fashion. He then revealed his left leg from underneath the bed sheets; the inside of his upper thigh was wrapped tightly with layers of bandaging. Nurse Foster removed the bandages and I tried not to look but couldn't resist peeking. There was a massive leg wound of unknown origin that consisted of all the colors ranging from red to pink, yellow to pus white. In large swathes it had turned black and marbled with shades of light greens and putrid browns. I gulped back a dry-heave and tried to only breathe out of my mouth to avoid the rancid smells which hung in the air like a noxious fume.

The nurse applied creams to the wound, made sad attempts at small talk with Gonzalez, and soon enough, we left. I locked both doors behind us as quickly as I could and considered my rounds, as well as her medication run, to be complete. But at what cost?

"Jesus," I muttered. "That was bad."

"Yeah, Gonzalez has been in that ISO chamber for a while now," she replied, pushing her stainless-steel cart back to the nurse's station, the wheels squealing every sixth rotation or so. "His wound is getting worse, and no matter how many times we treat it, it only gets worse."

"How is that even possible?" I wondered out loud. Surely modern medical science could handle a simple leg wound, even in prison.

"Well..." she started, hesitating for just a moment before continuing. "I'm not supposed to tell you this, but...he's been tampering with his wound. When we're not watching, he'll fuck around with it. Reinfect himself on purpose. No amount of ointment in the world will stop the infection if he keeps deliberately making the wound dirty."

I shuddered at the thought.

"What? Really?" I stammered. By now, I had internalized the desperation and depravity of the typical state inmate. Half of them were mentally deficient, and the other half were straight-up crazy. But even this sounded like a reach. "How?"

"Well, he uses his shit. Wipes it in the crevasses of the wound and..."

"Okay, okay," I interrupted. "I think I get it."

If the smell weren't enough to make me hurl, that information shared back in the room would have tipped me over the edge. But as I locked the last gate behind us and slumped back into my office chair along with CO Duran, my mind still hung onto Nurse Foster's words like an open wound itself.

"Why the hell would he re-infect his own wounds? With his own shit, no less?" I thought to myself, baffled by the phenomenon.

Duran finished his entry in the logbook, snapped it shut until the count, and turned the television on. The first thing to materialize was a weather girl. She was tall, slender, and as sexy as Nurse Foster but half her age. She daintily walked across the green screen and highlighted the temperatures for her 7-day forecast. 90+ degree heat for the rest of the week.

Suddenly, I had the answer to my burning question.

Gonzalez wasn't crazy at all. He was anything but crazy!

He was reinfecting his wounds so he didn't ever leave. Air conditioning. Television. A telephone all to himself! You would be crazier to heal up on schedule than if you milked the situation for as long as you could. He was disgusting, yet clever as a fox.

I put my feet up on the desk and sighed existential agony. Welcome to State Prison: where the inmates smear shit into their open wounds to capitalize on medical loopholes to avoid the discomforts of incarceration.

"Oh well," I said. "Hey, Duran? Put a movie on."

* * *

The United States healthcare system has been a hot topic for decades, and everyone, left or right-wing, seems to agree it's a broken mess. Everyone has an opinion on things like "single-payer," "copays," "preexisting conditions," and whichever talking point the media decides to whip up to keep the American public confused and distracted from more pressing issues. Is the system broken, though? It is, but the problem is so complex that even experts in the field aren't sure what to do about it, let alone an ex-prison hack like me.

But even though I might not be a stethoscope-wearing big brain, I can still recognize that the system itself requires a great deal of capital to keep it afloat. Medical professionals are, admittedly, highly-trained and intelligent men and women who deserve to be paid well for their necessary and challenging work. The profession also requires expensive medical equipment and medications to keep patients alive. Even a slight disturbance in that supply chain can cause disastrous ripples across the entire industry. The shortage of personal protective equipment or basic medical supplies during the Covid-19 crisis is just one recent example.

We can argue why our exorbitant health care spending achieves worse results than other countries, or debate the pernicious influence of Big Pharma (see: the Purdue Pharma-engineered OxyContin plague). But when it comes to prison medicine, it's an open and shut case. More specifically, prison inmates will, more often than not, have access to better, more expedient healthcare than the average law-abiding American citizen.

When your grandma or grandpa is sick, laid up at home with a disability or ailment that's too expensive to remedy, there is also an incarcerated individual simultaneously receiving an expertly-applied non-invasive procedure for pain while taking up a valuable hospital bed, manpower, and other resources in the process.

The prisoner's medical care is essentially free of charge. He will never receive a bill for that service, and if he does (which is rare), it will be so minuscule as to cover none of the actual services provided. Collection agencies will never harass him by mail and phone for the greater portion of his adult life. He will never be placed in the heartbreaking situation of weighing the pros and cons of sinking his family into insurmountable debt or simply giving up and dying.

In the world of prison medicine, men who have violated the social contract and betrayed the public trust receive healthcare completely on the taxpayer's dime. On the outside, these men and women would have stepped into a clinic or a hospital once or twice every few years. But in prison? These people, brimming with a sense of entitlement bred in them by the liberal counselors and medical professionals who work beside them, can score dozens of appointments per year!

In prison there are no co-pays, no deductibles, and no premiums. There is no limit to the amount of healthcare you can consume, and the gravy train is not just for crucial lifesaving medicine, either. Inmates receive free dental work from highly-trained doctors who are just as qualified to conduct their practice on the outside. They also receive free visits with optometrists for glasses, and ophthalmologists for any other vision-related issues. Whatever your ailment, and regardless of whether it was preexisting or incurred in prison, all work is carried out free, no questions asked. For many chronically ill people with thousands in medical debt, it might be wiser to commit a crime and go to jail for treatment! Once there, they could sit back and let the State administer the drugs and treatment for as long as necessary.

Sometimes inmates will go to the infirmary even when they aren't sick. Crafty convicts know how to drop key-words to a nurse during a check-up to gain admittance to the infirmary without much effort. Convicts will put on a big show over a stomachache or "chest pains" if they lose a bet and don't want to pay. By the time they get re-admitted to the block, tensions may have died down or the debt forgotten entirely. If an inmate commits too many block faux pas and draws too much heat from his fellow convicts, he can always make a medical escape for a few days, or even weeks, and strategize about what to do when he gets back. Meanwhile, the taxpayer's time, energy, and resources are spent trying to diagnose a ghost illness, all because an inmate wanted to scam his way out of taking responsibility.

But what's most infuriating about the prison healthcare system is how people on *both* sides of the political spectrum recognize its insanity...or at least would if they paid any attention to it. We are constantly barraged by valid claims about how bad *our* healthcare system is. The left of course wants universal access via socialized medicine (like in European countries), while the right warns about healthcare rationing, among other things. Meanwhile the incarcerated enjoy universal access with no rationing at all! It's the best of both worlds and none of the downsides.

In 1976, the Supreme Court ruled in the case of *Estelle v. Gamble*. The plaintiff, a prison inmate, claims he sustained back injuries while engaged in work within the prison, and Department officials acted "deliberately indifferent" to his medical needs.[23] Ultimately, the court decided in his favor, mandating that the Department's failure to provide "adequate medical services" to inmates was a violation of eighth amendment rights. Medical care for the incarcerated has been free or heavily discounted ever since (similar to illegal aliens receiving ER care they will never pay for). Some states do allow for a copay for services or a minuscule charge for medication. But these copays and fees are so ridiculously low the care is still essentially free.

Isn't that a bitch? Only in America can it be considered "cruel and unusual punishment" if a jail doesn't respond to your request for a free bottle of foot cream in a timely manner, yet somehow if you're a law-abiding citizen and suffer some calamity without insurance, you're shit out of luck. And don't forget, your tax dollars now also sponsor hormone treatment pills for degenerate felon perverts living a delusion. All it takes is for an inmate to claim "deliberate indifference" to his medical needs, and the prison administration will bend the knee in fear of a potential lawsuit.

The right wing will also fearmonger about waiting room wait times and overcrowded hospitals under socialized medicine. Conservatives love to blather about how packed our medical facilities will become if healthcare were to become free for all (while of course never doing anything about our unending Third World invasion). Once again, prison inmates typically bypass waiting rooms altogether, sometimes getting special entrances, facilities, or even entire wings of hospitals dedicated to inmates.

In New York, prisoners who are chronically ill can be transferred to a correctional facility which operates an RMU, or Regional Medical Unit. This ensures that no sickness, disease, or ailment goes untreated. Inmates with severe or urgent medical concerns or those requiring advanced medical procedures will typically be admitted to Albany Medical Center, one of the most prestigious hospitals in upstate New York. While it treats civilians, this hospital also operates a separate high-security ward devoted specifically to State convicts. NYSDOCCS even mans this ward as a permanent fixture of the Department itself. Untold millions of dollars are spent per year in not only healthcare costs but also on overtime and travel expenses

---

[23]United States Court of Appeals for the Fifth Circuit. *Estelle vs. Gamble.* 30 Nov. 1976. *Oyez.* https://www.oyez.org/cases/1976/75-929

for the Corrections Officers needed to transport and guard these convicts 24/7 as they undergo surgeries or various other medical procedures.

Not only do inmates sop up scarce medical resources like bread in a bowl of soup (resources that *should* be allocated for needy law-abiding citizens), but they also have prioritized access to it! While behind bars, the incarcerated man is apparently *superior* to Joe Public if the State's medical prioritization is any gauge. As a result, the average jailed murderer, rapist, or pedophile is likely to outlive the average citizen!

I do not advocate for dismissing inmate injuries incurred while incarcerated—quite the opposite. Any legitimate prison-incurred medical issue (assuming it's not self-inflicted) should be treated in a serious and timely manner by medical staff. That is not the issue. What I *do* advocate for is a rollback of taxpayer-funded medical procedures for prisoners which common citizens are not entitled to.

Inmates should not be receiving full dental work. Inmates should not be taking up prime real estate on an organ transplant recipient list. And above all, inmates should not be receiving sex change treatments at taxpayer expense. Their "transitions" are not medical necessities. They're not even real medicine!

Bottom line: if any working-class family is struggling with medical bills or any other medical access issue, no incarcerated criminal should be receiving better treatment. This is not immoral, nor is it brutal, bigoted, or mean. It's the common sense of a well-adjusted, sane person.

Extensive medical access for prisoners is more unfair to the working man than even their access to free higher education and professional legal counsel. They are privileges for common man, but rights for the felon. Anyone who pays taxes and abides by the law in this country should be furious at the audacious power dynamic here, and our politicians, judges, and media are equally complicit. What healthy society tolerates the advancement of the criminal class over the struggling citizen? What civilization has ever treated its prisoners better than its most vulnerable, including children?

The answer is none. No society or civilization has ever done this. And this is why we call it Clown World.

Americans no longer enjoy the benefits of citizenship or nationhood, thanks to the evil agenda of our hostile elite. We are instead far into dangerous new territory where everything is backward. We have crossed the Rubicon, leaving a world of normalcy and rationality to find ourselves in a land of insanity. This is a wicked place where the offender is lionized and rewarded for predatory behaviors, while those who guard him are demonized and punished for their efforts. It's a malignant blight on western civilization and a message of "DROP DEAD" to the average man or woman struggling to pay for treatment under the weight of farcical employer-subsidized medical benefits rotten with outrageous deductibles and premiums.

Inmate healthcare is so plush that many never want to leave the infirmary, unsettled gambling debts or not. Convicts will spread shit inside their own wounds to keep their room upgrades, and you pay for it. If insanity is defined as doing the same thing repeatedly but expecting different results, the prison medical complex is a prime example.

16

FIVE ROUNDS LOADED

*How using force is increasingly scrutinized
and shunned in favor of bargaining*

Migraines are the worst. They throb deep inside your brain like a miniature aneurism, and sometimes the pain is so bad you'd sooner take a 9mm round to stop the agony over a dose of Excedrin. On one fair September night as I sat watching the familiar faces of B-Block, an incredibly nasty one established itself inside my skull, and it refused to depart. It made an already miserable night much more miserable, and made me one especially surly Corrections Officer.

I sat at the officer's desk along with CO Lizak while nursing the pain. He was a golden child, the wise-cracking son of a beloved Sergeant, and he could thus do no wrong. But he was also a decent guy, a great officer, and never had a bad thing to say about anyone unless it was deserved. Even if he weren't the prison-equivalent of a college legacy applicant, he would have been a welcome addition to the jailhouse social order on his own merits. Regardless, we were both squinting through a pane of security glass and into the inmate TV room, trying to make heads or tails out of a hood-rat reality show the inmates had been riveted by for the past three weeks on BET. It featured tons of big-breasted, apple-assed females and plenty of urban dialects and ghetto couture thrown in for good measure. We had no idea what was going on, but we did what everyone working in a housing unit did at 7 pm. We watched the cons watching TV.

I quickly came to the realization that Lizak didn't join me on a boring housing unit just to hang out and watch ghetto soap operas. Quite the opposite. He was there to watch the block while I performed my nightly cell search. Officers in NYSDOCCS had to perform random searches on cells every day, and had about eight hours to complete them. But while they were being conducted, someone had to watch the rest of the unit.

"Lemme know what happens in this show," I said, as I stood up from the desk and walked toward the unlucky cell, my headache pounding away in a brutal cadence. "I'm dying to know."

"I'll spoil it for you!" he shot back, smiling. "The black guy steals a boombox, and his wife goes on welfare."

We both laughed.

My cell search that night wasn't intense, thank God. It was home to a small, rat-like convict named Veneración. He was a notorious crackhead who had a penchant for begging, borrowing, and stealing anything he needed; he used a shotgun approach when it came to getting over on security. His petty attempts rarely panned out, but he poked the bear so often sometimes he'd score a victory over an officer not wise to his cockroach powerplays. He didn't have much property, so scoring him on a random search was a blessing. The lack of stuff made the search much easier, and since I already knew where he hid all of his more "serious" contraband, I could cut the time in this little hole and save myself aggravation.

The search didn't take long. I walked out of it with a few state plastic garbage bags and mess hall cups, both considered contraband. While I wouldn't write him up for the infraction, getting it out of the inmate's possession was a small victory nonetheless. I walked back down the gallery to my desk, making sure to flag down the officer in the bubble to have him close the gate to Veneración's cell now that we were done with it. I turned around to sit back in my seat, and then...

"What the hell?" I asked aloud, noticing something strange on the ground, maybe four feet away from the officer's desk.

"What's up?" asked Lizak, half-interested as he watched the television with a pair of strained eyes.

"Is that what I think it is?" I pointed over to the floor, breaking Lizak out of his trance to get a better look. His eyes widened. "It better not be what I think it is."

On the floor was a small crimson trickle, three droplets of an unknown substance that could easily have passed for raspberry jelly if we weren't in a den of murderers. What was worse, a few steps away from that trickle was another. Then another. It continued like that for a few more feet, and after I realized that this was no case of someone dropping his PB&J, I turned to Lizak.

"That's blood," he said, getting up from his chair and adjusting his belt.

The hunt was on. Lizak and I scoured the ground of B-Block, following a trail of blood that weaved its way around the common area and up a staircase to the upper tier. I was the Shaggy to Lizak's Scooby-Doo, the only difference being whatever we were looking for was going to be far worse than any G-Rated spook protagonist in a cartoon from the 70s. Much, much worse.

The other inmates just sat quietly, hanging their heads low and pretending the unfolding drama didn't exist. They played cards, read newspapers, and watched TV. In reality, they were completely wise to whatever dark business just took place, and until now, we officers were none the wiser.

We followed what was now an alarmingly long trail of blood up the staircase and around the corner. Suddenly, the trail dried up, ending at the entrance to a shower stall on the upper tier. In the shower stood a fully dressed inmate with the water turned on hot, full blast. But more importantly, his face, which was homely to begin with, had been made less pretty by a pair of slashes cut deep in long streaks down his cheeks and across his acne-riddled nose. I recoiled at the sight. So did Lizak.

"Ramirez! What's going on? Are you okay?" I shouted, going for my radio. This wasn't something we could ignore. He had to go to medical, and fast.

"Eh, CO, I trip! I fell!" he stammered, whipping up the laziest excuse for his injuries he could muster. I didn't give him too much shit as he must have been in incredible pain, and as the shower turned off, the blood started flowing freely once again.

We hailed the Sergeant over the radio and began our walk back downstairs; most of the inmates by now were in rapt attention to the unfolding situation. Many of them feigned surprise at the sight of Ramirez and his diced face, but none actually cared. For them, this was merely drama they could pass around and consume for the next few days. Some couldn't contain themselves, laughing at the victimization of a fellow convict and energized with childlike giddiness at fresh bloodsports in their house.

Lizak prepared to walk Ramirez out of the unit and to the infirmary down the hall. But as we walked past the officer's desk, Ramirez snapped. The mocking tones and judgmental eyes from the inmates all around him grew too much to bear, and he took off in a monumental rage. Protruding from the pocket of his state-issued green pants was a thin, improvised weapon. It could have been a shank of some sort, but he was moving too erratically for us to identify it. He jerked the weapon upwards in a stabbing motion and broke away from us. Blood streamed down his face like an Aztec warrior possessed by the spirits of his ancient savage Gods. He wriggled past two inmates with a bob and a weave and ran through the door to the courtyard outside. He shrieked and shouted, and as soon as he got close to his target—a young, long-haired inmate of similar Hispanic descent named Burgos—he attacked!

Lizak and I pulled our pins, triggering a red alert on the unit. Our hearts beat in thunderous rapidity as we shouted at the two to break it up and stop the shit. Despite his advantage, Ramirez had difficulty connecting with his improvised shiv, and Burgos was doing more damage with his fists than Ramirez had bargained for. While we wanted to stop the violence, we also knew better than to tackle two violent men, one armed with an unknown weapon, without any backup. So we waited for the response team and hoped that when they arrived, the wounds sustained wouldn't be much worse than when they started.

Luckily, we didn't have to wait long. In an overwhelming wave of human flesh, the unit was suddenly beset by uniformed security staff members numbering over a dozen. They broke their way into the courtyard exterior and, with a coordinated rush, tackled the two convicts individually, making any sustained resistance impossible. I kept my eyes on the weapon Ramirez dropped to the ground. I stepped on it with a boot and made sure no other enterprising inmates could grab hold of it, whatever it was. The response team worked like a machine, holding them tight, and securing the scene. They were cuffed, and that was that.

In the end, Ramirez was punished. He was sent to the infirmary for his wounds and then disciplined for his assault on Burgos. He may not have intended to do so, but his attack revealed who slashed him in the first place. We didn't witness the initial assault, but why else would a convict suddenly lash out in such a targeted manner? This is how you identify a perp without being a rat. And it worked. About an hour later, Lizak returned to the unit to hang out, and we talked about everything that just unfolded. Soon enough, our eyes strayed back to the throbbing pulse of the television screen in the other room.

And my migraine? It was long gone.

* * *

Hollywood and the media machine that we feed with our attention and our wallets is a particularly odious type of cancer. Part propaganda, part racketeering, it's an industry that has thrived by bludgeoning our collective spirit for decades on end. Movies, books, magazines, music, and video games all serve as weapons of social engineering, and whether their play is obvious or subtle, if there's an agenda they want to thrust upon you, they'll seize the opportunity to do so. And chances are you'll pay full MSRP for the experience, complete with 3d-glasses and a large Coke.

The world of corrections is no stranger to the orchestrations of the media, either. It serves as the perfect backdrop for untold movies and television programs that depict Corrections Officers as baton-swinging apes and inmates as cherubic innocents unjustifiably targeted by their wrath. Who can forget the sadistic Officer Percy Wetmore from Steven King's *The Green Mile*, or any number of the corrupt or aloof guards from HBO's *Oz*?

These depictions, while entertaining on the silver screen, are bastardizations of a once-honorable profession. While writers, directors, and producers may create content knowing that their portrayals do not reflect reality, rarely can the consumer discern reality from fiction. Instead, Hollywood's fantastical lies get cemented in the cultural memory of the masses. After enough propaganda featuring the same narratives over a long enough period, *anything* can be demonized.

In reality, Corrections Officers might be one of the most scrutinized employees in the Western world, save for Police Officers or politicians. Instead of the brutish thuggery typically depicted, COs must resort to violence (or perform a "use of force" as it's called in the business) as an absolute last resort. Only when "de-escalation" and all other diplomatic strategies with an inmate have failed, can he swing his baton or use his fist. And if he does, it will be painstakingly examined and investigated for even a hint of excess.

The State of New York Department of Criminal Justice Services defines a "use of force" as force as "conduct which results in the death or serious bodily injury of another person. Serious bodily injury is defined as bodily injury that involves a substantial risk of death, unconsciousness, protracted and obvious disfigurement, or protracted loss or impairment of the function of a bodily member, organ, or mental faculty."²⁴ In the State of New York, whenever a Police or Peace Officer uses force in such a manner, it has to be reported. The same goes for the Department of Corrections and Community Supervision and agencies like it all across the country.

Use of force within NYSDOCCS is so regulated and monitored that every incident requires multiple reports to be filed in its wake. These reports, prepared independently and without collaboration between the parties, come from the Corrections Officer involved, the responding officers, and multiple supervisors. These reports are then forwarded up the chain of command and scrutinized at every possible level, with investigators and other departmental apparatchiks probing them for any holes, weaknesses, or blatant disregard for the liberal policies du jour. If the paperwork isn't a picture-perfect representation of the events that occurred at any moment, the relevant officer could very well find himself on administrative leave. He could also potentially lose his job, or even worse, come under criminal investigation himself.

To stem surges in use of force within facilities, NYSDOCCS established a concise rubric for using force. It ensures that Corrections Officers follow a specific procedure whenever an unruly inmate refuses to comply with a direct legal order. De-escalation and firm commands are mandated at the onset of any incident, but an officer can then resort to non-lethal methods such as pepper-spray or "departmental approved" body holds and strikes.

In corrections, you can't just go in swinging with bare fists like you're bare-knuckle boxing a drunk Irishman on the streets of Killarney. If you do, there's a good chance you'll get jammed up and shipped out. Instead, NYSDOCCS teaches a specific set of approved strikes, holds, and fighting techniques known as "defensive tactics." It's such a safe, politically-correct means of combat that even the name implies the user can never be the aggressor, merely the "defender." Usually, it involves a lot of manipulating the enemy's wrists, arms, and legs. It also includes a few methods to defend against oncoming strikes by inmates using edged weapons or fists. However, these methods are quickly forgotten by the average officer and never re-trained, unless he displays an interest in joining the Department's Corrections Emergency Response Team or "CERT."

Batons are also an option, but depending on the facility and how

---

²⁴ "NYS Crime Reporting." *NYS Division of Criminal Justice Services,* www.criminaljustice.ny.gov/crimnet/ojsa/crimereporting/use-of-force.htm.

comfortable an officer is in using it, he might not have access to one when needed. Due to the damage batons can inflict, they are more regulated than basic hand strikes, and if used improperly, the probability of getting sucked into some investigative clusterfuck triples. Batons were always optional in the facilities I worked, and I never felt the need to carry one. There were too many horror stories passed down by the older guys about what can happen if an inmate somehow gets his hands on your stick. I'd sooner rely on my own hands than risk brain damage at the hand of a drug-addled orangutan. I wasn't the only one who thought that way, either.

Whenever a nasty use of force situation arose, most officers pulled their pin and did whatever they could to survive the few minutes it took for a response team to show up. If survival meant throwing a few right hooks or using an improvised weapon, so be it. Paperwork could always be written to make the incident appear to be a "life or death" situation, which was an easy-out for those in an actual severe situation. But no one ever wanted to be in that situation. Everyone wearing a blue shirt just wanted to finish their shift, go home, and be spared the red tape.

After non-lethal force options are exhausted, the next fallback in the rubric is *deadly* physical force. This involves the use of firearms, and if you have access to firearms in a correctional setting, chances are you're already pretty well versed in what to do and what to expect. Guns are not common tools behind bars; they're highly secured in a facility's "armory" and are only given out or deployed to highly-controlled secure posts, usually outdoors and remote from inmates altogether. Tower posts are normally armed, and during my time as a CO, I worked in a tower quite often. These little sniper nests are usually outfitted not only with a radio, comfy swivel chair, and a mini-fridge to chill your lunch but usually have directives, policies, and the use of force rubric displayed on the wall for quick reference.

As a tower officer, I was always prepared to work with and coordinate with other tower officers, mobile units, and officers on the ground if use of force was required. Take the yard, for instance. If a fight, riot, or escape attempt kicked off, or if a fellow officer was swung upon, it was within my right to announce my intentions over a loudspeaker and rack a round into the chamber of my weapon. By then, if the hint wasn't taken, I had full authority to deploy that weapon and drop the convict. I was justified to deploy deadly force. I just better not miss.

We had a few options to do this, too! NYSDOCCS trains its

officers in a trio of weapons, each with unique strengths and specific training regimens. The most common, and the one required to qualify with to keep your job, was the Glock 17 pistol. When I joined the NYSDOCCS, we were still trained using old Smith & Wesson .38 revolvers, and while they were fun, the Glock was far more practical. These weapons were issued to all armed posts and were expected to be used to defend you or other, more critical, state-issued equipment such as vehicles or heavier weapons nearby.

Second was the Remington 870p shotgun. This loud, wood-handled beast was rarer than the Glock and much more situational. It was great for crowd control, and its tell-tale "clack-clack" sound it made when you chambered a round was usually enough to stop a fight in the yard through audio authority alone. We were trained to use this weapon with two kinds of rounds, buck and bird-shot, but the powerful boom and righteous kick we got from each round was the same.

Lastly was the department rifle, the Colt AR-15. While it may have a reputation as the preferred choice for mass shooters and the perennial target of gun-grabbing Democrats, the rifle itself proved to be an incredible tool. ARs were issued to tower posts mostly, or anywhere with a clear vantage point over a large area where inmates might congregate. Unfortunately, because the tool had the capacity to cause significant damage to the inmate population, NYSDOCCS restricted its use and limited its power artificially.

By reducing the number of rounds that could legally be held in its magazines, trigger-happy officers had to pause to reload a new magazine more often than a common citizen at a rifle range. They issued us thirty rounds of 5.56 ammunition, but they had to be loaded into six different magazines! "Five rounds loaded into a box-type magazine inserted into the rifle" was the mantra the Academy instilled on range days, and it was one of the few pieces of practical information that carried over into everyday use. My time in the tower involved setting up the weapon for what was known as "wall tower storage." It was a practice that left COs a weapon safe yet ready to fire at a moment's notice. Failure to prepare the rifle correctly could cost precious moments in a time of crisis, so we made sure to follow the steps to the letter for the sake of our fellow officers.

No matter the type or caliber, all firearms were available for the specific tasks of preventing murders, escapes, riots, or damage to state property. Luckily, I was never in a position where I had to discharge any of these weapons, but not every Officer is so lucky. If a lethal force situation did arise, our trainers always instructed us to stay calm and fire at the "center of mass." This meant no head-shots, crotch-shots, or disabling blows to legs, knees, or arms. This reduced the risk of instant death or permanently maiming a target, but also prevented shots from careening wildly into a nearby crowd or an unintended target; a torso was big enough to be considered safe. That said, it wasn't always a sure thing. If for certain situational realities an officer did have to fire at an inmate's head or extremity, he could do so as long as the paperwork afterward reflected that he fired at the center of mass. The State and their investigators can't always account for wild movements made by targets, and if a nappy head happens to bob or weave into a round's trajectory, well, then it sucks to be him.

If a situation remains out of control despite the use of firearms, then the final option is to deploy chemical weapons. NYSDOCCS relies heavily upon CS tear gas, available in various grenades and delivery systems, and primarily stocked in yard areas and larger mess halls. Corrections Officers can only deploy tear gas if he needs to stop serious damage to state property or to prevent escape. Otherwise, deployment of chemical agents is typically reserved to the level of Watch Commander and above. But if it gets to this point, the situation is probably so FUBAR that the grenade launchers are loaded and ready to fire at a moment's notice.

As mentioned previously, any use of force triggers a tremendous amount of paperwork. If an officer hits anyone, shoots anyone, doses anyone with pepper spray, or even if he shoves an inmate in a slightly aggressive manner, it can be considered a use of force depending on the situation. When these things happen, everyone in the vicinity must file an independent report, with no coordination and completely un-coached by supervisors. This causes nerves to run high. If any report deviates even slightly from the rest, it can cast a shadow on all of them. A state investigator can easily spin one utterly justifiable incident into one where the Officers were the bad guys looking to pick a fight with a pitiable convict.

I've witnessed this unfortunate scenario. A fellow officer was once assaulted by an inmate under the influence of the dangerous opioid Fentanyl. The officer's face was shattered, and as he lay on the ground writhing in pain, the response team closed in just in time to save his ass. The inmate was forcibly subdued, and eventually taken to the infirmary to be processed. After the smoke cleared, one of the officers in the response team was coached by a well-meaning yet bumbling Sergeant as to what to write in his report. The officer obliged. The report ended up a horrid and contradictory mess, and the Department then crucified the officer in a lengthy disciplinary process, and he was ultimately terminated for taking the Sergeant's advice. The other officers were even investigated by the FBI for their involvement in this particular incident, but did they do anything wrong? Absolutely not. They lawfully showed up to defend a fellow brother in a life-or-death situation!

To minimize situations like this, some facilities (but not all) use video surveillance cameras to record housing units, corridors, and other major arteries within the prison. If things pop off and go south, the camera footage is used as physical evidence of the incident. Many officers bitched and moaned about being recorded. Many didn't want to be seen slacking off, cursing, or talking trash about the brass or other officers. But I've always been a major proponent of their use. It keeps officers honest, and when push comes to shove, the videos *will almost always* exonerate them. Consider body-cams on police officers. Whenever community outrage at a police shooting or instance of "brutality" breaks out, the body-cam footage almost always paints a different picture to show that the officer's actions were at least partially-justified. The same is true in correctional facilities.

The last thing officers should want is a use of force with nothing in the aftermath but a bloody convict and a lot of hearsay. In those circumstances, written reports reign supreme, and they're far too malleable and subject to human error. Once an investigation starts on the basis of words on paper, it becomes your word against an indigent, presumed-innocent inmate. Good luck with those odds in today's victim-lionizing society.

Far more often than not, video footage saves your job, and maybe even keeps *you* out of a jail cell. Thankfully, some departments have begun to unroll body cameras for Corrections Officers, and the cameras are welcome additions to an officer's everyday carry. I never had the luxury of one myself, and during my tenure these cameras were rare to the point of rumor and legend. Not every facility is as modern and well-funded as others. Budget cuts often hit departments hard. Even in New York, where prison funding is considered generous compared to other states, camera coverage is sparse. With the exception of SHU units, perimeters, infirmaries, and other critical areas, the average facility is entirely lacking in video coverage, leaving you to work every day essentially naked in the Wild West.

Violence occurs almost every day in corrections, leaving good men and women subject to pillory by the State just for enforcing its own policies. Since the State is overly concerned by public opinion and swayed too easily by the media and threats of civilian lawsuits, it constantly changes policies to suit the needs of politicians. It will enforce insanity even if it means the termination of innocent Corrections Officers in the process. If a policy is followed to the letter of the law but ultimately leaves an inmate so injured that the media or conniving lawyers catch wind, it will dramatically tear down and replace that policy in knee-jerk fashion. It will unveil a new one in its place, usually confusing and counter-productively stifling, without any time to test it or ease it into the Department as a whole. This leaves Corrections Officers always on edge, second-guessing every action they make, and sometimes, too petrified to use force at all! Instead, the State opts for submissive behaviors like bargaining with problem inmates to keep the peace.

This cowardice, this lack of authority in the men and women expected to serve the public trust, is an untenable situation. How can a peace officer keep the peace if his superiors are continually shifting the tectonic plates of policy underneath him? How can a law enforcement officer act with confidence in his actions if he is not confident his superiors will support him, or the offending inmate he is squared up against? How can a violent situation be quelled if an officer doesn't know if the punch he's about to throw will save his life or ruin it, resulting in termination from the force?

Painfully often I witnessed COs sit down and stay quiet when an inmate broke a rule or caused a significant problem...even little violations that didn't require the use of force to begin with! The men and women working the blocks of prisons across the country are overwhelmingly neither weak, lazy, nor stupid. They *mean* well and have the capacity to *do* well. The problem is not that they *won't* do the right thing to discipline an inmate, but they feel that they *can't* without being punished from above. They don't feel confident in their authority, and that is caused solely by the State's shifting use of force policies and politically-correct management. The brass is always looking to keep "use of force" numbers down for their respective facilities, and the Departmental promotion of "de-escalation" tactics to deal with problem inmates is dangerous.

Violence is, in itself, a form of de-escalation. If you use a baton to stop an inmate from crushing someone's skull, then you de-escalated that situation. Had you not, things might have escalated to the point where a victim's brains lay spilled over the mess hall floor. Words might be pretty, and they might save the State from lawsuits, but they don't keep people safe from violent maniacs, and they won't keep correctional staff safe from rampaging lunatics. If anything, de-escalation is a destructive tactic, placing Corrections Officers at risk and in positions of weakness. Authority is undermined the second petty bargaining begins.

So while *Orange Is the New Black* might depict prison guards as complete troglodytes, and *The Shawshank Redemption* might show officers beating inmates within an inch of their lives just for crying at the gate, the reality is far from the depiction. The true average Corrections Officer is a man or woman frequently on edge: scanning crowds of violent convicts, mindful to grab not a baton, but a radio for backup. Officers lack the professional confidence needed to maintain performance for the twenty-five years duty before retirement. Officers never know if a tour will get them fired for a picayune infraction, no fault of their own, or if that sad scenario is just postponed another day.

Until officer authority is restored to a rational level, and there is institutional support for use of force situations, the alarming lack of real security in our correctional facilities will only grow more dire as the years progress. The mission statement of the New York State Department of Corrections and Community Supervision is to "ensure public safety by operating safe and secure facilities." But what if staff can no longer uphold that basic premise? What if they are no longer able to provide the care, custody, and control needed to perform in a fair, firm, and consistent manner?

What results is the situation we have now. Every Corrections Officer is a potential convict the second he has to implement his own department's policies. These men and women should be proud of their profession, but instead shuffle their way to and from the time clock filled with dread, mistrust, and bitter loathing of a career they nevertheless feel indefinitely married to. They are like battered housewives, aware of the brutality of their paymasters, but too afraid to liberate themselves.

What results are men and women doing twenty-five to life.

Eight hours at a time.

17

THE GOLDILOCKS ZONE

What must be done to maintain the public trust
and improve the lives of both correctional officers and inmates

The ancient Greeks would famously speak about the Lernaean Hydra, a terrible beast forged by the Gods with only one purpose: to slay the son of Zeus, Hercules. The Hydra, who lived within a deep cave inside the swamps of Lake Lerna, was capable of terrible things. It could breathe fire, devastate villages, and its veins pulsed steadily with thick, poisonous blood. But the most cunning of all of its dark powers was its ability to sprout many heads. When one was cut, two emerged to take its place. This left the hero, Hercules, with a perplexing task. How do you kill a monster with so many heads?

The tale of the Lernaean Hydra is painfully analogous to the American correctional system. While it may not breathe fire, it does have many heads, all of which are terrible and capable of tremendous damage to the innocents all around it. It too lives in deep, impenetrable caves, and until it is faced directly with the courage and bravery of strong, indomitable men, it will continue to wreak havoc on a nation which continues to enable its existence.

Simply put: The Hydra must be slain.

This will be no easy task. The correctional system features many failures, each representing one of the Hydra's many heads. Each of these must be lopped off and cauterized to prevent it from growing back. But while Hercules had ten labors set before him by his enemy Eurystheus, we, good men and women of the nation, have but one in this case. And that is what makes our victory possible.

No one gains from the current correctional order. While departments across the country might uphold their task of keeping the incarcerated away from public view, they do so in a way in which the convicts reap every benefit. They are lavishly spoiled with electronic gizmos and free healthcare, while hardworking families on the outside struggle to afford care for their own maladies. At the same time, however, convicts *do* suffer. They are fed an abysmal poison of industrialized slurry, allowed access to near-limitless amounts of mind-numbing pornography, and forced to share spaces with some of the most psychotic and criminally insane people the nation has to offer. They are placed in a sort of emotional limbo, with any joy derived from the softer nature of our criminal justice system erased by that same system's many inconsistencies.

The public gains nothing from the current order, either. While it may be satisfied to be temporarily rid of criminals running amok on the streets, it is entirely unaware of the many benefits those same criminals receive once incarcerated. The convict grows fat and complacent, and his standard of living actually *improves* behind bars. Once inside the general population, he is reunited with old friends and gangster colleagues, where he is offered a safe environment in which to hone his criminal skills. He is provided all the legal tools necessary to chip away at an already weakened system from within, and those tools are provided free of charge by powerful, affluent opinion-makers and our subversive intelligentsia. While these urbanites offer unwitting convicts diplomas, legal representation, and a bevy of other privileges with a smile, these creatures of modernity merely use convicts as pawns in their game of bourgeois status-climbing and performative peacocking. They virtue signal to other progressive social circles while spitting on the common man in the process. The result of this transactional power dynamic is tragic: the criminal's behavior is never actually corrected, and his prison no longer serves as a deterrent to crime. Instead, his behaviors are rewarded and his criminal skills enhanced, leading to more crime upon his release.

With this broken, subverted system, nobody wins.

Nobody, that is, but the system itself.

Thus far this work has detailed the many failures, hypocrisies, weaknesses, and insanities within American correctional institutions, using NYSDOCCS to illustrate them. But this chapter will be different. Instead, it is dedicated to solving these problems. It includes a series of demands that must be met to reestablish trust between law-abiding civilians and the prison departments tasked with correcting criminal behavior. It outlines clear measures that must be taken to properly rehabilitate criminals and cease the erosion of the institutional authority needed to maintain proper control of its many facilities and penitentiaries. Ultimately, it details how to establish a Correctional "Goldilocks Zone," a system that is not too soft, but not too hard. Instead: just right.

This metaphorical sweet spot can only be established by adopting bold, reactionary ways of thinking as to how we should view the profession of corrections, whether in local, state, or federal jurisdictions. Once adopted and maintained, the reverberations of such changes would be felt throughout communities across the nation. Crime would plummet, criminals would truly be reformed, and the many men and women who work within these departments would be able to do so again with heads held high.

There's no better place to start than by addressing the place where correctional careers begin.

#1: The Academy.

For Corrections Officers, the Academy should be where positive, practical learning takes place. It should instruct officers in the institution's values, the tools required to do the job, and the esprit de corps needed to operate within high-stress environments. Officers are often told that the Department of Corrections is a "paramilitary" organization. But if Academies in their current form teach us anything, it's that these learning centers offer only a cheap facsimile of military life. In reality, it's a prolonged gym class mixed with extended human resources meeting. From the outset, recruits are filled with wrong ideas about predatory old timers and fat slugs who refuse to get off their asses to open gates or issue commands. From the get-go, the cadet is taught to hate his future co-workers before he ever meets them, and is thus set up for failure before even arriving at his first post. This foments an instant aura of mistrust between new officers and those with seniority. Academy courses themselves are also abysmal. A recruit is taught more about all the ways he can be terminated from the force than he is about what to do in a dangerous situation.

I propose a complete re-working of the Corrections Academy: if the profession is to be considered a paramilitary organization, it needs to be run as such. Recruits must be screened more intensely. They need to be far more carefully picked and pruned from the population to prevent those with criminal sympathies or any connection to street gangs from sneaking through. A stringent entry exam needs to be implemented across all departments, perhaps uniformly at the federal level, to filter out those with low intelligence or behavioral pathologies. The profession is a tough one, and those with weak temperaments should be excluded from service. The current testing regime is either too easy or, in some cases, non-existent. NYSDOCCS eliminated entrance examinations for State Correctional recruits, and opened the flood gates for bad actors as a result.

Physical fitness tests and overall standards need to be elevated as well, and PT of all categories *must* be emphasized. Things like parade drills are done only to prepare recruits for one big show at graduation, never to be performed again. I propose that drill (marching and moving as a unit), gain greater prominence in the training rubric. While it may appear simple or of dubious efficacy, it has been the building block of western militaries for centuries. Its rigorous use in training led to notable victories for men like Napoleon, Wellington, Caesar, and Jackson. Correctional officers too can learn from its ability to instill greater morale, discipline, and esprit de corps.

The same must also be said about "defensive tactics." A completely new martial art system should to be introduced to correctional officers, one effective enough to work in a prison environment but also simplistic enough to teach and train recruits *en masse*. It has to be taught not only during the Academy, but also at regular intervals throughout officers' careers—perhaps yearly, just like weapons qualification. This will keep martial arts prowess consistent for all officers. In the event they themselves one-on-one with a hostile inmate, they must be capable of deploying a strike or a blow in self-defense or to enforce compliance with a direct legal order. And they need physical confidence and competence to be effective.

Lastly is the training itself. Those who teach recruits need to know the job. They should be men, ideally with seniority, who have extensive experience working the correctional beat and who can teach practical lessons to the young men and women who will one day replace them. These officers must also be rotated, lest they become complacent and removed from the job they once mastered. Placing instructors in classrooms for limited tours would ensure that recruits are always being taught by individuals who worked in a housing unit recently. In my experience, men with time on the job have a lot of wisdom, and a half-hour conversation with one of the older officers was worth an additional eight weeks in the Academy. What we have now are classes run by men and women seeking an "easy-out" of correctional duties, opting for teaching roles in lieu of rounds on a housing unit.

We must also remove the political correctness endemic within the curriculum. There is no reason why week-long blocks of instruction should be dedicated to sexual harassment or "racism in the workplace" when a single class at the beginning of the Academy would suffice. Every minute spent teaching officers to hate themselves and be wary of others' actions is a minute that could be spent on practical skills or policy. The current system not only undermines the "paramilitary" ethos the State pretends to instill, but it's also a liability to those who intend to work the career nobly and effectively.

Ultimately, we need to train healthy, confident, and upright men, and infuse them with the necessary authority to carry out their duties. The Academy is where this must begin. Which brings us to the next topic.

#2: Restoring authority to the Corrections Officer.

Corrections Officers are law enforcement officers. While their powers vary by locality, they are all proud, badge-carrying members of a police or peace officer organization. They all serve the public trust, and as a result, need the authority to do their jobs and keep their workplaces safe for *everybody*.

Disciplinary procedures for workplace wrongdoing should be standardized across the board. If an officer betrays his fellow officers or the trust of his wards by smuggling dangerous contraband like weapons, drugs, or outside technology, then he needs to be punished for it. The same should go for provable instances of brutality and excessive insubordination of lawful direct orders. These punishments should be quick and efficient, delivered in a way to prevent further damage or disruption to befall the Department.

That said, petty infractions like bringing in magazines, newspapers, or even glass Tupperware or mason jars, should no longer be entertained as even a *possibility* for disciplinary action. Corrections Officers are entrusted to protect the public and other inmates from harm and injury. If they can be trusted to man a sniper's nest with an AR-15, and authorized to shoot a firearm and end a human life if they deem it necessary to do so, then they should also be trusted with things like non-clear lunch bags, coolers, and pieces of uncooked meat. They should be treated with the respect and dignity earned by a member of law enforcement, not treated like toddlers in a playschool. They must no longer be the unwitting victims of the State's inadequacies and wrongdoings, scapegoats for bureaucratic failure.

The same rational policies should also apply to security supervisors. Sergeants and other lower-end management staff should have the freedom and authority to run their units and areas as they see fit. If a Sergeant and his subordinates want to proactively police a facility via aggressive searches, developing confidential informants, or just following up on leads from concerned members of the inmate population, they should be empowered to do so without constant pressure from above to "lay down" or "stop making waves." This feminine culture of dissuading initiative because it might become "problematic" is a wildly dangerous one. It hamstrings proactive policing by lazy, cowardly higher-ups. This laissez-faire attitude toward festering issues creates a dangerous atmosphere in correctional communities and serves to make them unsafe for *everyone*. They grow rife with unchallenged infractions, gang activity, drugs, and violence. In the end, any rosy quarterly reports mean nothing if the officers and inmates are living the opposite of what it portrays. Good, honest work should always be rewarded and never punished. Brave initiative should be embraced, not shunned.

On the whole, we must reestablish a proactive and sane power dynamic in corrections, returning authority to law enforcement and out of the hands of the complacent bureaucrat, conniving criminal, and corrupt politician. The profession still rests on a foundation of treating inmates in a fair, firm, and consistent manner to maintain care, custody, and control. With a little bit of common sense and a lot of elbow grease to set this "Goldilocks Zone" in place, officers will be more motivated, prisoners better treated, and the public safer overall. Opponents to these measures will only reveal their hand: a devious, evil agenda to punish the good and law-abiding and reward the selfish, violent, and outright evil.

#3: Inmate classification and the return of the death penalty.

True order and protection cannot exist in a prison if there is mingling between violent and non-violent offenders in the general population. While the current systems allow for sorting inmates into different categories based on offense history, program eligibility, and medical needs, many times these lines are blurred and bad apples fall through the cracks. The inmate classification system must be completely re-worked so that it keeps the mostly inert general population quarantined from violent murderers, rapists, psychopaths, and other severe defectives.

Face facts. There are many non-violent inmates who simply made a mistake or ran afoul of the system, and have been sentenced to time by a judicial system with its own perfidious agenda. (The pro-white advocates strung-up after being assaulted in Charlottesville come to mind.) Men like these, nothing more than political prisoners, should not live perpetually in fear while behind bars, wondering if their bunkmate or neighbor will explode into an inexplicable murderous rage at any moment and randomly shiv them for a perceived offense. All violent offenders should be segregated in separate facilities, isolated from the vulnerable sad sacks who may have made a wrong turn in life somewhere. It's not rocket science to tell the two types apart. Violent populations should be classified as anyone sentenced for murder, assault/battery, rape, or found guilty of similar acts while incarcerated for a different offense. These facilities would be wall-to-wall monitored and staffed by willing corrections veterans capable of dealing with the worst of the worst. Violent cons would be separated into smaller, more manageable housing units of 20 men or less, with little intermingling between them. The facilities would feature holding pens built to neutralize savages, replete with the infrastructure to execute the worst of the worst of the worst.

And yes, I said execute. The death penalty has been an option in Western criminal justice for the overwhelming majority of our history. It must be accepted in the national conscious, and judiciously used! While some states still practice executions, and the federal government has only recently re-entered the arena, the process is barraged continuously by activist lawyers and legislators, causing capital sentences to be dragged out for years (often decades) in slogs of unjustified bureaucratic red tape. We need a nationwide re-adoption of the death penalty, and any illegitimate procedural barriers to execution effectively removed. Not only would this prevent the unforgivable from becoming lifelong taxpayer burdens, rotting away in the general population to grow fat and entitled, it would also re-establish a centuries-old deterrent to violent crime in the first place.

As it stands, Capital punishment in the modern day only ever seems to be plied, and lauded, when it is used against white offenders. While these criminals should not be saved from their fate, nor should their horrid actions be excused, it should be noted that applying lethal force to end the life of a violent criminal is only ever truly acceptable when it's done against someone with European ancestry. When a white man is on the chopping block, there is no parade of pro-bono lawyers seeking to filibuster his execution for six decades, and there are no racial based political groups available to champion his cause on an ethnic level. As a result, our judicial system operates totally unabated when up against white criminals, while it stalls and chugs along when the offender in question happens to be a misunderstood "person of color" or some other protected class. Don't believe me? Well the evidence doesn't lie. When politicians like Donald Trump and his Attorney General William Barr reinstated Capital punishment, as they did in the summer of 2019, the first to die were indeed white men. In fact, out of the first six inmates to be put to death under President Trump's new commitment to execution, five were of European descent.[25]

Another correctional issue which must be addressed is the mentally-ill or the criminally insane. It is one of the great tragedies of this once-great country that state mental health institutions have largely shuttered their doors to those in desperate need of proper mental healthcare.[26] Hospitals, prisons and correctional facilities have carried the burden ever since, often housing inmates who simply don't belong there. Mentally-ill men and women should not share spaces with the sane. The only thing that keeps them from erupting into regular psychopathic episodes are cocktails of drugs dealt by terrified nurses behind a plexiglass window. These drugs are often controversial or come with dangerous side effects, capable of wrecking the recipient's psyche even worse than it was before medication. When they fail (and they often do), the sane inmate suffers the consequences. This is yet another prison tragedy, and it prevents rehabilitation of sane inmates who should be spared such nonsense. It shouldn't be allowed to continue.

To spare the ordinary inmate from the insanity of the mentally

[25] Khaleda Rahman, et al. "These Are the Inmates Executed during the Trump Administration so Far." *Newsweek*, 9 Dec. 2020, www.newsweek.com/inmates-executed-trump-administration-1553498.
[26] Ruffalo, Mark L. "The American Mental Asylum: A Remnant of History." *Psychology Today*, Sussex Publishers, 13 July 2018, www.psychologytoday.com/us/blog/freud-fluoxetine/201807/the-american-mental-asylum-remnant-history.

ill, we must expand America's psychiatric institutions. The non-violent criminally insane, who suffer greatly from the current machine's inadequacies, need intimate and proper care from qualified mental health professionals, and the country's correctional facilities are woefully ill-equipped to deliver that care. What we have now are holding pens for transient lunatics and a system barely capable of shouldering the burden without imposing disastrous results on the rest of the population. If we expand asylums across the United States and improve their level of care, these individuals can be adequately treated, and we can watch as the number of violent outbursts or "unusual incidents" within our correctional facilities plummet to record lows.

#4: Reestablish a healthy, self-sustaining prison food program.

When you think of a meal in prison, thoughts of gruel, slabs of mystery meat, bread, and water usually follow. And that's not Hollywood programming. Prison food is manufactured to meet State-determined, bare-minimum nutritional guidelines and tightwad bureaucratic budgets. The results are horrible industrialized dishes, steam-cooked in a bag, and served to frowning faces all over the country. But it wasn't always this way!

Decades ago, food in prison was decent and healthy. Fresh vegetables and grains were grown on the prison grounds and prepared in large elaborate kitchens. Prisons would own and operate extensive, self-sustaining farms complete with livestock pens, butcher-shops, and bakeries. The food would then be served fresh to the inmates daily. Due to the quality of these freshly cooked meals, the inmate population was not only happier, but they gained practical knowledge and rewarding experiences in the process.

There's no *good* reason why food served to the incarcerated man has to be disgusting and soul-crushing. But nevertheless, it is.

I propose a complete restoration of the prison food programs of yesteryear. By allocating land in or near correctional facilities for cultivation and reopening prison farms across the board, we can feed incarcerated men healthy, delicious meals capable of keeping disgruntled sentiments to a minimum and help ease them back toward civilian life. This provides the dual benefit of providing new, fulfilling jobs and programs to teach inmates valuable skills during their stints. They can learn to farm, work the land, and understand concepts like animal husbandry and the preparation of traditional home cooked meals. They can join a baker or butcher program, and by the time they are released, their resumes would be filled with practical skills capable of elevating them to meaningful employment outside.

The age of meals conjured in industrialized vats and stuffed into plastic bags for re-heating must end. It teaches inmates nothing, save for how to feed mouths in a mass-controlled setting. These brutalizing methods and processes are not highly sought-after skills by employers on the outside. Instead, we must work to stop this corporate, mass production of prison slop and instill a positive, healthy nutritional program capable of filling bellies with good food and filling minds with the abilities to exceed in life after prison.

#5: Shift to a pro-active healthcare system, and establish equity with the taxpayer.

The sanctity of life, even for the convicted felon, should always be upheld. No one should writhe in pain while dying a slow death behind bars, nor suffer from ignored injuries sustained while locked up. However, the current system allows for far too much manipulation by the incarcerated. Inmates submit for "sick call" for every little tummy ache, sprained toe, or headache. They complain incessantly, scamming their way into privileges like special "diet meals" or assistive canes, which are more for status signaling and pimp-limping among their homies than used as actual crutches. At best, they clog the already overburdened American healthcare system with elective surgeries and procedures, and at worst, they hog spaces on organ transplant lists, potentially robbing innocents of their more-deserving treatment.

This madness has to stop.

I propose an overhaul of the inmate medical system. While access to healthcare should be available to the incarcerated, and doctors should still be expected to uphold their Hippocratic oaths, the burden of such costly procedures should be shifted away from the taxpayer and back onto the inmate. Convicts should have to pay copays and medical costs, just like civilians, charged for each and every visit to the infirmary. These costs should be controlled and scaled to match inmate wages, and they should never come free of charge. Doctors and nurses working behind bars should also have the authority to report or discipline inmates in instances where they might be lying to receive frivolous medical attention. This would deter inmates from unnecessary treatment and improve legitimate care in the process.

Alternatively, we could adopt a socialized healthcare system in America, making healthcare free and available to all, with all hospitals and clinics run by the state. But since the chance of that happening in the next decade or two is slim at best, it is easier for the civilian to demand equity with the incarcerated, however it is implemented.

I also propose that physical fitness, through workout regimens, organized sports, and other exercise programs, be not only expanded in correctional facilities but mandated. Nothing puts an inmate in a healthy state of Zen faster or more effectively than sports. Whether watching his peers play basketball, football, soccer, or participating in them himself, sports are a positive and active way to strengthen the mind and body. By hiring outside civilian or military physical fitness trainers and organizers, inmates can expect to participate in all forms of weightlifting or bodybuilding pursuits. By improving access to games, equipment, and the time needed to engage in such activities, the incarcerated man can truly improve himself. He can opt to improve his physical form and discover healthy and positive outlets to release pent up aggression and hostility toward authority.

Transsexual inmates and other sexual deviants will no longer be rewarded with special treatment. The days of the public shouldering the mentally ill's quests for hormone therapy, sexual reassignment surgeries, and various other bodily disfigurements will finally conclude. No longer will the state pay for or maintain an inmate's "transition" from male to female (or vice versa), and no longer will it enable delusions of gender-based grandeur. Instead, it will provide resources to treat instances of body dysmorphia in healthy, positive ways. If necessary, these mentally-ill individuals will be transferred to mental health institutions better suited for their restorative needs.

#6: The removal of pornography, temptation, and smut.

Masturbation, while not explicitly banned in correctional facilities, can result in a write up or a trip to SHU if an inmate is suspected of "exposing" himself to others purposefully. But let's face it, sexual frustration and the aggression that follows are potent forces and is no better demonstrated than by the convicted felon. During his incarceration, a man will go through emotional torture due to his lack of access to the fairer sex and the pleasures he once enjoyed as a free man. To cope with this sudden loss, he will embrace vigorous masturbation via the world's most degenerate pornography. If his urges are still not satisfied, he might even indulge in same-sex activities with his fellow convicted men. By then, a man has crossed the point of no return. Once these former taboos become the new normal, he will often continue to march beyond the pale into sexual depravities that would horrify the most jaded Weimerican.

These Satanic transformations are a tragedy in themselves, and can be prevented with one simple act: the complete abolishment of pornography from correctional facilities.

While it may seem harmless or even beneficial as a pressure release valve, prison pornography is the first step on a slippery slide into utter sexual depravity. When combined with a convict's vast amount of free time, the over-consumption of such material profoundly harms the psyche. Banning such material is an essential reform, and this includes nude photographs sent by wives and girlfriends on the outside, which are often freely traded to other inmates, without remorse or dignity, for other jailhouse comforts like tobacco or snacks.

If we can categorize porn as contraband at the same level as drugs or alcohol, then we can begin to stop or slow the downward spiral of inmates addicted to the material and of masturbation itself. We can also expect to see reductions in prison rape and sexual activity by wide margins. Since pornography acts as a degeneracy accelerant, removing it from facilities will prevent men from growing numb to its temptations and stop them from seeking satisfaction directly from their peers.

To fill the void left by lack of degenerate material, inmates should turn to their own families, friends, and relationships on the outside. While incarcerated individuals already have access to visitations and family events sponsored by the prisons and other inmate led groups, these programs should be expanded to allow the maximum amount of quality time with loved ones. I propose additional family days, holiday events, and other positive, family building get-togethers that inmates can enjoy and use to create and maintain healthy connections with their families. These events, of course, will be entirely based around an inmate's disciplinary record and classification. Still, those who qualify can expect to serve incarceration in a positive, wholesome, and healthy manner that benefits not only the inmate but his family who eagerly await his release.

On the other hand, homosexual and transsexual inmates, or those who display homosexual behaviors while incarcerated, need to be removed from general populations and placed into separate, secure units. By separating these individuals from inmates who want to carry out normal, wholesome sentences, we reduce the risk of both consensual and non-consensual intermingling between the two. These inmates, who for the sake of easy classification can be referred to as "LGBTQ," will have all of the resources available for them to carry out sentences of their own, safe and far away from other, more violent and predatory inmates. They will even be offered mental health resources to steer them away from the path of suicide or self-harm and back onto the path toward healthy recovery from traumas they may have experienced while incarcerated or throughout their lives back home.

I also propose that those who *do* commit rape be disciplined in the severest possible fashion. These inmates should be transferred to facilities explicitly designated for violent offenses. Along with pedophiles and other sexual offenders (especially those whose victims are minors) these people should be considered candidates for chemical castration. Those who betray the trust of society in such inexcusable ways can only be dealt with physically. If the death penalty is not an outright option for their specific case, then castration is a second-best alternative. It should be used judiciously but without remorse.

#7: Re-locate prisons and modernize their infrastructure.

The United States is full of natural wonders. It has vast mountain ranges, emerald green forests, shimmering deserts, and golden fields as far as the eyes can see. It has rivers, valleys, foothills, swamps, and long, sandy shorelines.

Unfortunately, it also has correctional facilities, behemoth dens of societal decay, dotting every rural landscape imaginable like a case of smallpox. They operate far and away from the major cities in which most inmates originate, while they typically recruit officers and other security staff from local towns and counties. What results is a sick symbiotic relationship, where ruralites are paid mercenary wages to deal with urbanite problems.

To spare the wondrous landscape of this country from further marring of its natural beauty, and to inoculate the country from this particular sickness, we should close, condemn, and completely demolish prisons in remote rural locations. The land these dark constructs occupy is too rich and too wonderful to be left in the grip of departmental bureaucrats to house our worst. If we were to remove them, the land could be restored and repurposed in the service of natural beauty and the preservation of rural locales.

That is not to say these prisons should be closed and not reopened somewhere else. Quite the opposite, in fact. They should instead operate closer to the urban sprawls which generate the need for them in the first place. Like New York or Los Angeles, cities are often filled with wealthy individuals or powerful elites who do their best to keep prisons far and away from their own backyard.

No more!

By constructing new, modern prisons complete with advanced security, tactically-sound architecture and floor plans, and the means to house inmates of all classifications, these new suburban or city-based facilities will be better able to accommodate the convicted felon and the communities that grew him. While prisons like New York's Sing Sing may be culturally significant, their construction is ancient and would be better used as a museum like Alcatraz than as an actual correctional facility. By allowing these dangerous places to remain open, and at full capacity no less, we only endanger society and enable attempts of escape by crafty inmates seeking to exploit breaches in decades-old infrastructure (as demonstrated by the 2015 Clinton Correctional Facility escape).

These new facilities should also be outfitted with advanced, all-encompassing video surveillance equipment. No area of a facility should go without camera coverage. By completely wiring a prison and all of its corridors, housing units, and various other rooms and chambers for both sight and sound, we can ensure both inmate and officer accountability 24/7. They will also have modern computer equipment approved for officer use and able to track, monitor, log, and categorize inmates, inmate groups, and their typical behaviors. These databases will be in secure locations and will have internet access blocked for security purposes. All correctional officers could have access to them to examine pre-loaded files and folders, including departmental directives, facility policies, and communications from management or supervisory staff. Access to such technology establishes a level of parity between other, more public-facing law enforcement agencies and correctional departments, which often struggle to keep up with advancements widely available in other fields.

#8: Prevent those with self-serving interests access to the minds of incarcerated men.

There is nothing more enraging for the average working man than seeing a criminal gain more in prison than he can ever hope to gain outside of it. As it currently stands, a criminal can not only earn free healthcare, but also gain access to a college-level education completely free of charge. This is made possible by non-profit organizations that weasel their way into correctional departments using private donor money and usually under the guise of progressive platitudes. Inmates can even continue their taxpayer-funded education upon release. In doing so, they have cut the line and bypassed the high price point set by educational gatekeepers that ordinary working people struggle to surmount.

Inmates never pay a dollar in tuition; they never worry about buying books or paying exam fees. It's all free, and offered with a smile. This is the height of hypocrisy. It is an abomination to the idea of the social contract, and for its crimes against sanity this practice must be stopped.

I propose that NGOs and other third-party inmate advocacy groups be barred entirely from prisons. If a civilian has to be buried under mountains of student loan debt or become an indentured servant in order to attend college for any reason, an inmate should not be able to bypass these obstacles. Period. By removing these groups' access to incarcerated men, we can block the shortcut they provide criminals to educational success that everyday people will never see. We can also prevent wealthy urbanite elites from using inmates as their playthings, as pawns in their game of status-seeking, ladder climbing, and virtue signaling under the guise of progressive "philanthropy." The incarcerated man does not deserve the help of the Wall Street millionaire; he needs only the corrective methods instilled by the Department of Corrections, or at the very least, one that actually corrects behavior and maintains a proper correctional "Goldilocks zone."

I also propose that we prevent these same types of non-profit groups from giving inmates access to pro bono legal aid! How many times has a civilian been wronged by a business, company, workplace, or individual but failed to produce the capital needed to engage in a legal battle to right the wrong he suffered? Well inmates don't have these problems, as they have lawyers and other ambulance chasers tripping over their own feet at a chance to win a big one in the name of social justice! By removing access to these free outside legal resources, we prevent inmates from practicing lawfare and prevent the death of the institutions that hold them. We prevent the erosion of departmental order, stop inmates from becoming entitled after legal victories, keep authority in the hands of security, and uphold the sense of justice a victim's family receives when these criminals become incarcerated.

No more loopholes.

No more privileges.

No more retreating.

Incarcerated men must simply face the music and take accountability for their actions.

Now, you might be asking yourself, "How the hell can we do all of that?" Admittedly, it's a lengthy to-do list. How can anyone expect to achieve such grandiose, sweeping reforms amidst the current neoliberal order our Correctional institutions face? Well, it's going to be a lot of hard work, a lot of self-sacrifice, and a lot of fighting to get the job done. But in the end, the Corrections Officer, supervisor, or civilian who might be reading this book right now all have the tools necessary to pull it off.

You have to get mad. Get loud. Make noise. You must continuously flex your political power and never cede an inch of ground! Never give up the attack, and most importantly, if you already work in one of these Departments, you must...

#9: Demand a redress of grievances, or strike!

You have to understand that the things being demanded in this book are not crazy. They are normal demands, made by many normal people in response to a completely abnormal system. The desire to punish a criminal for his misdeeds and to right the wrongs he made against society is a normal impulse and the reason we have a criminal justice system in the first place. But when the criminal justice system in a society no longer carries out the will of those who have been wronged, and instead offers privileges to the incarcerated as if they were the everyman's better, we can no longer rely on that system to uphold the public trust.

Instead, we must demand these non-negotiable changes and force a return to normalcy. This can only be done by concerned citizens and the efforts of organized labor. In an ordinary world, prison staff could go to their union and demand these changes through democratic means and by leveraging Robert's Rules of Order. But the unions, which are rife with corruption, personality cults, and career bureaucrats only looking for an easy twenty-five, are more concerned with derailing smart workers with red herrings than fighting any battle that will bear significant fruit. They operate merely as a dead-end, or an off-ramp for a furious membership fooled into thinking they're enacting changes. All the while labor leaders collaborate with management behind the scenes to keep the gravy train rolling.

No more.

If correctional officers want to see changes on the job or see the pendulum swing back into their favor, they're going to have to strike. They're going to have to strike hard, fast, and decisively, with or without the union's blessing. It's going to be difficult, especially in States where striking is illegal (New York, for instance.) But no good has ever come without sacrifice. No victories were ever gained through big talk and a soft hand.

You're going to have to stand outside every day for weeks, maybe months on end, shouting at traffic by the roadside. You're going to have to heckle every suit-wearing member of management that drives by and remind him he's nothing more than a political opportunist and a traitor to his men. You're going to have to warm your hands by barrels of fire and eat whatever food gets passed around the picket line. Worst of all, you're going to have to denounce and bully the State Troopers and National Guard they call in to replace you. They'll be scabs after all, and they need to be treated as such.

But you'll have to endure the pain. You'll have to endure the financial suffering just a little longer to make a change in this world. And only when it seems like you can't possibly take it any longer, and you start doubting the whole point of this strike, they'll come to you with an offer. And you'll have to be prepared to turn it down even if it's enticing.

That's because you, a champion for the working class, should never accept anything from the enemy that isn't total surrender. You're facing down the Lernaean Hydra, after all. But always understand: they cannot fire all of you. Corrections departments across the country are already starving for manpower and survive only on a trickle of recruits per year. It's barely enough to man all of the housing units and various posts within the average facility, and as crime skyrockets across the nation, this demand will increase. These departments also grow more and more liberal, opening new programs, events, and posts. With the constant shuffling of inmates on transport buses and vans day in and day out, the Department increasingly relies on officers for everything yet consistently gives back less and less.

But take heart! You are in a position of power. By striking, you not only demonstrate to management that you are sick of their unsafe policies and unfair pay, but also to the elite that puppeteers our society that you will no longer tolerate the manipulation of your once-hallowed institution. You're not just fighting against the career-driven brass that runs your facility. You're also sticking it to millionaire politicians, the university intelligentsia, and the corporate elite, all of whom march lockstep in unity with the convict held high as their banner. All it's going to take to bring the system to its knees is one prolonged wildcat strike, and you can be the men to do it finally.

Your average correctional department is already fighting a two-front war with constant pressure mounted from pushy, entitled inmates and outside watchdog groups. It's continually ceding ground in a world that grows more progressive by the day. I say we open a third front in this battle of ideas. With a membership that marches in solidarity against the radical changes that have been foisted on them year after year, we must stand together and demand our own set of prison reforms.

We must demand *sanity*.

We must demand *justice*.

We demand *fairness*.

We must demand that Correctional Departments be held accountable for their actions and that they *actually* begin to correct inmate behaviors as their name implies.

We demand they offer workers a dignified wage, and most importantly, we demand the implementation of a correctional Goldilocks zone. One that's not too tough and not too soft, but just right.

18

ONE FOR THE ROAD

An epilogue

In prison, holidays were always the worst. The shifts seemed twice as long, the nights twice as cold, and everyone seemed three times more bitter than they usually were. But this was understandable. Spending eight hours or more in a correctional facility away from your friends and family while the world came together without you makes a man want to get up and punch a concrete wall.

It took all of my energy to hold that fist back one Thanksgiving night, and as I walked the gallery on B-Block, I watched as snowflakes fell gingerly onto the courtyard outside. Once they hit the ground, they gathered in small white clusters, which soon spread until they covered the pavement in a sheet of thin, shimmering snow. "Dammit," I thought. "It's going to stick."

I had already worked a full eight hours that day, and by the time the snow began to fall, I had a whole 'nother eight in front of me. It was my fault, though; I swapped with a day-shift officer so he could get time off to spend with his kids. It was a ritual I had performed every year, like clockwork for both Thanksgiving and Christmas. Selfless, sure, but I didn't see the need to have those days off for myself if I didn't have a family to enjoy it with. It only made sense to share the goodwill and liberate the older guys, even if it was just for the day. Besides, they worked for me during the days I needed, so it was mutually beneficial.

"McKraken to the console. Repeat, McKraken, to the console."

A voice blared out over the unit's loudspeaker. It was CO Wannamaker. He was a young hotshot officer who had garnered a reputation among the older COs for being cocky and a loose cannon around convicts. It turns out a lot of the rumors were bullshit. The guy just liked fast motorcycles and hot women. He was rambunctious; he talked a mile a minute and drank way more coffee than humanly possible. It didn't help that he had a baby-face and a habit of bouncing his leg up and down in fits of limitless energy. By the time I got to the window, he looked through the small glass slit and smiled at me, laughing like a hyena.

"Hey brother, what's happening, man?" he cackled. I was one of the few guys in the joint that talked to him on the regular. For all of his high-octane intensity, I understood him and where he was coming from. Behind the young-punk veneer, there was a smart, good kid. I engaged him as an equal, unlike most of the old-timers. After hearing all of the different rumors and stories relating to Wannamaker, I figured out what their problem was: They ran out of spunk like his years ago, and they envied him for still having it.

"I'm tired," I replied, resting my arm on the edge of the bubble window, while the other reached in and grabbed a cup of piping hot java. Since Wannamaker was the bubble officer tonight, he was the one in charge of making the unit's coffee. I was in luck. The guy would keep pots brewing until an hour before shift change.

"Me too, bro, me too," he shot back. "Last night was drinksgiving. Bro! I didn't get back home until 5 am. Got like one hour of sleep, and then the alarm went off. Now I'm here."

"Holy shit," I groaned. "I don't know how you do it. You must be shot."

"Yeah," he said, smiling. "It's all good, I got coffee, and we're almost half-done, bro. Easy money."

"Amen to that," I replied, taking my coffee and giving it a slow swig. On holidays, the prison was run with a skeleton crew of young guys comprised mostly of swappers who, like Wannamaker and me, promised to help out older guys with getting the day off. You also had a small segment of officers who didn't have families or prior commitments; they were typically middle-aged outcast types who might have been through a divorce or two. The kind of guys whose Thanksgiving dinners would consist of a Hungry Man and the television cut of "It's the Great Pumpkin, Charlie Brown." Lastly, you had the unlucky guys who couldn't find a swap and were now stuck here due to their own lack of diligence. While they were the most miserable, they usually didn't stay long. Most facilities would often approve extra time off on holidays, and at most, these men would have to stay at work for a few hours before they could cut loose and spend the rest of the day off on vacation time.

This meant that the inmates didn't get to enjoy many of their usual programs, classes, or scheduled work details, but that's okay.

Most of the time, they were completely fine with staying in their cells, maybe coming out to watch TV for a while or playing a game of cards before calling it quits. It was almost an unspoken rule that you didn't fuck with officers on holidays or make any extra work for them. It was hard enough to have to be here in the first place; there was no need to aggravate an already grumpy officer and make the situation worse for the whole block.

But what made the holidays special was that it was one of the only times that we officers could really celebrate. Our facility operated a little jailhouse potluck dinner every year, with each officer approved to bring in food that everyone could share in a giant feast. Some guys brought in desserts, some brought whole turkeys, and some covered the condiments, napkins, forks, spoons, and Stove Top stuffing. Entire trays of the stuff would be stacked in our line up room upfront and kept warm in mess hall hot boxes rolled down from the kitchens. After inmate chow was served and things settled down, officers were called up front to grab a plate and bring food back to their post. Everyone got to go up, sometimes twice, and everybody ate. It was a rule.

It wasn't long into my second shift before the bottom tier lights flickered off and back on again. I knew what that meant: The Sergeant was coming. Good bubble officers would flick the lights to give you a heads up when supervisors were walking, and this was Wannamaker's way of letting me know he was worth a damn.

Instinctively I kicked my feet off the desk, stood up, and walked over to the main gate out of the unit.

It was Sergeant Dave, the red-faced Irishman who covered A and B blocks tonight. Just like us new guys, he was stuck at work on a major American holiday, and now he was on my unit all the same. I said hello and prepared to walk a round with him, as was correctional tradition, but instead, he merely smiled and waved me away.

"Hey, McKraken!" he said with a big smile and a pair of crossed arms. "Listen, I got the block covered for now. Go head up and get some chow."

I smiled back, gave him my keys, and thanked him for the relief. This was not an orthodox move for a Sergeant by any stretch of the imagination, but I was happy he swung by. I zipped up my coat and began the walk up front, which if done at a brisk pace, took only a few minutes at the very most.

By now, in my career, I knew this particular facility quite well. I always had a knack for directions, but even so, this prison was relatively small, and I learned the layout of the place before I was even out of on-the-job training. But that night, I could have been completely blind and still found my way up front, using only my nose as a guide. I followed the wafting scent of home-cooked treats down the corridors until I finally made it to my destination. The line-up room was usually bare and bereft of any amenities. Still, that night, it was loaded with happy people, almost indistinguishable from a Country Kitchen Buffet or Golden Corral.

Mountains of food sat in neat rows before me, with more pies, cakes, cookies, and freshly baked bread than there were officers on duty. On one end, you had all the meat you could imagine, sorted by the animal, and on the other, you had every carbohydrate you could ever conceive. Potatoes, sweet potatoes, mac and cheese, corn, carrots, rutabaga, stuffing, cranberry sauce, green beans, and beansprouts. You had pork, chicken, turkey, and roast ham. White, wheat, asiago, brioche, and challah bread and enough butter to grease down a grown man. There was so much food it was intimidating. When one wants to eat everything, where does one start?

Luckily, I wasn't the only one facing this dilemma. Upfront along with me were about ten other officers who all got a relief to cover them while they hit the buffet. We did what any big group of hungry men and women would do, and we formed a line. With Styrofoam trays in hand, we moved like a machine, filling up on food at each little station until our trays could barely close without mashed potatoes or gravy-soaked stuffing spilling out the sides.

While we stocked up on potluck goodness, we were also cracking jokes and laughing. We were telling stories of years past and smiling all the while. And despite some of us being locked in that terrible place for up to sixteen hours, somehow, we were merry. Sure the food was excellent, but the fact that we could all come together despite the dark, sometimes dangerous situations our profession placed us in gave us a sense of contentment.

We were all co-workers, but more importantly, brothers and sisters bound to each other and sworn to protect our own. What we were experiencing that Thanksgiving night was the warm, comforting embrace of camaraderie, of real *esprit de corps*, and although it was rare, we cherished it while it lasted. We never knew what was in store for us tomorrow. We never knew if we would finally be the target of an inmate assault or live out the worst-case scenarios we all knew might happen one day. We never knew if we would be the victims of departmental senselessness and lose our jobs due to some arcane policy or procedure. We never knew if our lives were going to change at the drop of a hat.

But in that moment, we could ignore all of the uncertainty and dread. In a brief, precious respite, we could smile and relax. We had good food and good times. We had each other: all friends, family, men and women alike.

Just livin' the dream.

www.ingramcontent.com/pod-product-compliance
Lightning Source LLC
Chambersburg PA
CBHW021632120626
46545CB00002B/507